How to Shoot from the Hip Without Getting Shot in the Foot:

MAKING SMART STRATEGIC CHOICES EVERY DAY

How to Shoot from the Hip Without Getting Shot in the Foot:

MAKING SMART STRATEGIC CHOICES EVERY DAY

James D. Stein, Jr.
Herbert L. Stone
Charles V. Harlow

John Wiley & Sons

New York · Chichester · Brisbane · Toronto · Singapore

Copyright © 1990 by James D. Stein, Jr., Herbert L. Stone, and Charles V. Harlow

Published by John Wiley & Sons, Inc.

All rights reserved. Published simultaneously in Canada.

Reproduction or translation of any part of this work beyond that permitted by Section 107 or 108 of the 1976 United States Copyright Act without the permission of the copyright owner is unlawful. Requests for permission or further information should be addressed to the Permissions Department, John Wiley & Sons, Inc.

This publication is designed to provide accurate and authoritative information in regard to the subject matter covered. It is sold with the understanding that the publisher is not engaged in rendering legal, accounting, or other professional service. If legal advice or other expert assistance is required, the services of a competent professional person should be sought. *From a Declaration of Principles jointly adopted by a Committee of the American Bar Association and a Committee of Publishers.*

Library of Congress Cataloging-in-Publication Data

Stein, James D., 1941–
　　How to shoot from the hip without getting shot in the foot: making smart strategic choices every day / by James D. Stein, Jr., Herbert L. Stone, Charles V. Harlow.
　　　　p.　　cm.
　　Includes bibliographical references.
　　ISBN 0-471-52219-8
　　1. Decision-making.　2. Human information processing.　I. Stone, Herbert L., 1939–　.　II. Harlow, Charles Vendale.　III. Title.
HD30.23.S7257　1990
658.4′03—dc20
　　　　　　　　　　　　　　　　　　　　　　　　　　　　　　90-11906

Printed in the United States of America

90　91　　　10　9　8　7　6　5　4　3　2　1

Dedicated to:

CSH	Leslie	Krista
KJT	Brian	Karrie
		Lauren
		Jonathan

Preface

Processing information intelligently is frequently the difference between correct and incorrect decisions. To illustrate this point, consider the familiar story of the person who lost a watch on a dark street one night and is foolishly looking for it not where it was lost but under a streetlight, where the light is better.

Is this really foolish? It depends on what information is known. If the person has information that enables him or her to localize where the watch was lost, it is obviously ridiculous to look elsewhere. On the other hand, if no such information is available, looking under a streetlight is an intelligent strategy because the watch is just as likely to be there as anywhere else; however, it is much more likely to be *found* if it is in a place where the light is good.

Defining the problem and specifying the relevant and irrelevant information are critical parts of solving the problem. An approximate solution to a well-defined problem is much more useful than a well-defined solution to an inaccurately defined problem.

Business managers are subject to a flood of solicited and unsolicited information, both relevant and irrelevant, which often results in information overload. Information overload can produce a kind of mental fibrillation that dramatically reduces the efficacy of the decision process.

The solution to information overload is to filter irrelevant information and condense relevant information. In order to filter irrelevant information, a manager must learn to recognize and utilize the dominant variables, those affecting the success or failure of the strategic choices that must be made in a given business environment.

How to Shoot from the Hip Without Getting Shot in the Foot presents a model for filtering and condensing the information needed to make good decisions in a competitive business environment. Importantly, the model simplifies reality without contradicting reality. Bite-sized scenarios describe an environment and offer three choices. On the back of each scenario page, the reader will find the solutions page, which provides a brief analysis of the choices and the principles involved, along with point values assigned to each choice, which measure its efficacy. The final condensation of the dominant variables for each scenario appears at the bottom of the solutions page in a section called "The Bottom Line."

Some scenarios stress making good decisions; some emphasize avoiding bad ones. Sometimes the reader has an opportunity to be brilliant; sometimes the best outcome is simply to avoid disaster. Even the best decision makers cannot spin gold from straw, but good decision makers must be able to recognize what is gold and what is straw.

How to Shoot from the Hip Without Getting Shot in the Foot is divided into eleven chapters. Each consists of a section entitled "The Issues," which supplies an incisive overview of the topics to be treated in the chapter, and a number of scenarios. A caveat: The time the reader spends with "The Issues" will be richly rewarded, not only because of their immediate value in analyzing the scenarios but also, more importantly, because of the long-run value that results from becoming sensitive to the dominant variables inherent in major management and marketing problems. As the reader cultivates a taste for the dominant variables, he or she will also be learning how to recognize information that is not useful—a capacity devoutly to be desired.

The reader will find out soon enough that the authors are firmly convinced that learning can be enjoyable and that the processes of filtration and condensation need not interfere with the pleasures of learning.

It's time to begin. Turn to the first chapter and read "The Issues." Then read the first scenario and select the one option that seems best. Turn the page and read the analyses of the possible choices, remembering that it is often possible to learn as much or more from analyzing incorrect choices as from analyzing correct ones. Progressing through *How to Shoot from the Hip Without Getting Shot in the Foot*, the reader will notice that the processes of filtration and condensation become more natural and that it becomes easier to make right choices—for the right reasons.

The reader has an opportunity to measure his or her progress at the end of each section and again at the end of the book. While it is enjoyable to do well in a game situation, it is far more important to make a commitment to learn to recognize and utilize the dominant variables and the principles that govern them. This ability is critical in determining the success or failure of strategic choices in a competitive environment.

Acknowledgments

Obviously, everything we've read and experienced is part of us. It is impossible for us to acknowledge the contributions that many have made to our present state of thought. We do, however, acknowledge our indebtedness to Michael Porter, whose seminal work at Harvard has contributed a robust model of the competitive process.

We are grateful for the many useful comments and suggestions from colleagues and students at California State University, Long Beach, especially colleague Dan Madison, whose trenchant comments significantly improved the original manuscript. Many thanks are due to reviewer Brian Forst of George Washington University for his constructive suggestions and comments.

John Mahaney, our editor at Wiley, and his capable, cheerful staff were constant sources of encouragement. We would be remiss if we failed to thank the score of companies who helped us focus on the issues and answers we write about.

Finally, the authors must confess that they thoroughly enjoyed developing an entertaining structure for learning a lot, too often an improbable combination.

Contents

5

Strategic Groups, Barriers, and Industry Evolution

The Issues   *109*

So How Are You Doing?   *137*

PART III   THE INDUSTRY AND ITS MANY PHASES   **139**

6

Coping in a Fragmented Industry

The Issues   *141*

7

Industry Growth, Maturity, and Decline

The Issues   *153*

8   Strategies for International Markets   193

PART IV   SOME MAJOR DECISIONS   207

9   Vertical Integration   209

How to Shoot from the Hip Without Getting Shot in the Foot:

MAKING SMART STRATEGIC CHOICES EVERY DAY

PART I

Decisions, Dominant Variables, Strategies, and Actions

1

Decisions, Rewards, Risks, and Dominant Variables

THE ISSUES

Strategies: Rules of Action

It is often stated that you have made a good decision if the action you have chosen leads to a favorable result. However, the outcome on a particular occasion does not tell you much about the efficacy of your rules for making decisions. One or a few favorable outcomes can occur even when a poor decision process is used. If the rules governing decision making are poor, sooner or later the law of averages will exact its inexorable toll.

Good decision making involves developing strategies, rules of action, that lead to generally favorable outcomes over a reasonably long period of time. For example, two different strategies frequently pursued by businesses are the low-cost producer strategy, in which the business tries to produce the item or service at a lower cost than most of its competitors, and the narrow-market focus strategy, in which the business tries to produce the item or service custom-tailored for a particular collection of buyers. These two strategies may well specify different actions, even under the same conditions, yet both strategies may lead to long-term success.

Developing rules for good decisions requires examining the actions available and choosing the one with the most favorable payoff. Even the determination of the most favorable payoff requires care, as this might be the one with the greatest long-term gain in some situations

3

or the one with the least immediate exposure to risk in others. Without short-term survival, a priority for fledgling companies, there may be no long term over which to maximize the gain.

Whenever you can estimate the payoff from each possible action with a fair degree of certainty, it is generally relatively easy to make a good choice. However, if the payoff also significantly depends on actions taken by others, such as competitors or customers, then your choice becomes more difficult because you must take into account their probable actions, a variable over which you have minimal control at best.

Dominant Variables

Some variables, such as customer preferences or competitors' possible actions, may have a large impact on the payoff, whereas other variables have a lesser effect. Those variables that have the largest impact are *dominant variables* and should be considered seriously when you evaluate your possible decisions.

The business world is sufficiently complex that it is impossible to devise a strategy that caters to every possible combination of all relevant variables; the number of such combinations can be astronomically high. However, by considering primarily the possible combinations of the dominant variables, one can reduce the number of possible combinations to manageable proportions and also make sure that the combinations with the greatest possible impact on performance are the ones being considered.

When determining the dominant variables, it is extremely helpful to know

1. who you are (your strategies, strengths, weaknesses, etc.)
2. who your competitors are
3. where you are (what kind of industry and competitive environments you face).

Although this information by itself will not guarantee favorable decision making, it is a necessary condition. To prosper, a business needs a clear picture of where it wants to go, and it needs to know the potential obstacles to its success, including an assessment of the probable actions of its competitors, suppliers, and customers, as well as the payoffs associated with its own possible actions.

Scenario # 1

Sweet Victory

As head of Consultants R Us, you have been hired by a fledgling food producer that has come up with a sensational new candy bar that actually prevents tooth decay. It's hard to imagine a product with a greater appeal to kids, except possibly vegetables that taste like chocolate. The food producer has a number of in-house experts who have helped develop the product, but it has decided to invest in outside help to locate potential bottlenecks. Sending them the right expert will help embellish your own reputation; you want to be sure that this product makes its way into the hearts and stomachs of American children. Should you send them

▶ **A**

An advertising expert, to make sure that the company does an effective job of bringing the candy bar to the public's attention?

or

▶ **B**

An expert on manufacturing processes, to make sure that the company gets off to a good start by manufacturing its product in an efficient manner?

or

▶ **C**

A marketing expert, to make sure that outlets for selling the candy bar can be found?

⟶

Solutions #1: **Sweet Victory**

A An advertising expert, to make sure that the company does an effective job of bringing the candy bar to the public's attention?

▶ **3 points** A truly great advertising campaign can make up for a multitude of sins. If the advertising campaign is especially effective, the demand for the candy bar may be so great that outlets can more easily be found.

B An expert on manufacturing processes, to make sure that the company gets off to a good start by manufacturing its product in an efficient manner?

▶ **I point** Although it is always important for a company to get off to a good start, in this case a manufacturing expert is unlikely to make a significant difference in the production of the candy bar, especially considering that the in-house experts have probably studied this particular problem closely to the exclusion of all others.

C A marketing expert, to make sure that outlets for selling the candy bar can be found?

▶ **5 points** The crucial problem is most likely to be finding a place from which to sell the candy bar. A visit to the supermarket or any other place where candy products are sold is quite likely to reveal shelves crammed with an assortment of products from such heavy hitters as Hershey's and Nestlé's. Breaking into the starting lineup is liable to call for substantial ingenuity, perhaps even selling it at dentists' offices, and this is the weak point at which an outside consultant is most likely to help.

Score _____

━━━━━━━━━━━━━━━━━━━━━━━━━━━━━━▶ **THE BOTTOM LINE**

On the plains of commerce bleach the bones of countless products that died for lack of adequate marketing. A chain is only as strong as its weakest link, and marketing is often the weakest link in the merchandising chain.

Scenario #2

On Location

There are few sounds quite as compelling as that of a laser cannon successfully blasting an enemy spaceship out of the sky, unless it's the sound of a child pleading with a parent for another quarter so that he or she can play, "Just one more game, pleeeeze, Mommy!" This is of course the reason that you and a few friends have decided to pool your resources and take a flyer in the video games industry. You would love to be able to conduct a market survey to determine optimal locations, but you have just been offered a very attractive opportunity to get into the business because of a forced sale situation. The vendor is giving you the first shot at taking over some of his machines, but he wants an answer within hours, otherwise he'll look elsewhere. You'll certainly get an edge by taking advantage of his distressed prices, but should you

▶ **A**

Rent a number of machines and place them all in the same location?

or

▶ **B**

Purchase one or two machines and place them in the same location?

or

▶ **C**

Rent a number of machines and scatter them throughout different locations?

⟶

Solutions #2: **On Location**

A Rent a number of machines and place them all in the same location?
▶ **1 point** Not a bad idea, especially if you happen to hit a primo location on the first try. However, what if you don't? You could find yourselves in the horrifying position of having made a winning decision to enter a profitable industry but having ruined it through faulty execution.

B Purchase one or two machines and place them in the same location?
▶ **–2 points** This is a classic example of how to do everything wrong by putting all your eggs in one basket. Admittedly, if you do everything right this may maximize your profits in the short term, but what happens when the particular machines you purchased are no longer popular? Renting machines may cut into your profit margin, but you don't have to worry about asset obsolescence, which can be severe in an industry such as this one.

C Rent a number of machines and scatter them throughout different locations?
▶ **5 points** This approach figures to prevent you from scoring the biggest possible gain at the start, but whenever you start a business you want to learn while you earn and vice versa. By placing different machines in different locations, you will in effect be conducting a market survey, and when the time comes, you will be much better placed to make a decision as to where to locate. The dominant variable for this enterprise is location, and it is important that you identify the best locations early and diversify to minimize your risk.

Score _____   **Running Score for Part I** _____

━━━━━━━━━━━━━━━━━━━━━━━━━━━▶ **THE BOTTOM LINE**

Initial diversification with respect to your dominant variable can move you up the learning curve rapidly and with reduced risk. The period when animals and companies are most vulnerable is shortly after birth.

Scenario #3

Opening Number

They say there is no such thing as a guaranteed product winner, but you and several friends of yours feel that no one could get closer. Your group consists of top-notch engineers, salespeople, and marketing experts, and you have developed a high-definition technology for television, which generates a picture as sharply defined as film. Your salespeople have been talking to both industry and the government, and they are confident that the ink will be dry on the contracts long before you even have a product you can ship out the door. The important questions revolve around ownership, risk, and financing. Should you

▶ **A**

Retain all the ownership and start small with low risk, borrowing a small amount from your friendly banker?

or

▶ **B**

Retain all the ownership and start large with high risk, creating great leverage by borrowing a large amount?

or

▶ **C**

Start large by getting all of the risk capital from investors by giving up 45 percent of your ownership?

➡

Solutions #3: **Opening Number**

A Retain all the ownership and start small with low risk, borrowing a small amount from your friendly banker?

▶ **1 point** Although your growth may be slow because you are starting small, you are assured of keeping control. The chief drawback is that there is a very good chance that your competitors will come up with an improved version that costs less since they can produce it in volume.

B Retain all the ownership and start large with high risk, creating great leverage by borrowing a large amount?

▶ **3 points** You are a favorite to win big, and if you do, you get to keep it all. However, any delays or miscalculations could be disastrous because of high fixed-interest costs.

C Start large by getting all of the risk capital from investors by giving up 45% of your ownership?

▶ **5 points** This choice gives the company both the lowest risk and the highest probability of success. Not only that, but if success occurs, the company's 100% equity base will allow it to borrow large amounts quickly should expansion be desired. Choices B and C are superior to A because they result in a larger scale of operation, and this is a situation in which undercapitalization can greatly reduce your probability of success. The choice between B and C is determined by your attitude toward investment risk, but the reward/risk ratio of option C is higher. If this situation presented itself to you many times, by choosing option C, sooner or later you would be bound to succeed, but an early failure choosing option B might prevent you from ever getting back in the game.

Score _____   **Running Score for Part I** _____

━━━━━━━━━━━━━━━━━━━━━━━━━━▶ **THE BOTTOM LINE**

Just as an atomic bomb will fail to detonate if the critical mass of fissionable material is not present, a company can fail to succeed if a critical mass of assets is lacking. It is not enough simply to get off the ground; you want to stay airborne.

Scenario #4

In Fashion

Happy days are here again for Dinah's Designers, a small midwestern chain of boutiques specializing in high quality dresses, which are produced elsewhere to Dinah's Designers' specifications. You have guided the firm from one small store to the point at which you now have retail outlets in Chicago, Detroit, and St. Louis, and have grown steadily during the past few years. You have recently been approached by an outside firm offering expansion capital, and the board is currently meeting to consider three different ways of utilizing this money. This is a critical period, and you want to make a flexible move that offers good upside prospects. Should you

▶ **A**

Invest in a small factory, reducing the cost of manufacture by keeping the entire procedure in-house?

or

▶ **B**

Use the capital to expand by setting up additional outlets in other midwestern cities, such as Minneapolis and Omaha?

or

▶ **C**

Establish an outlet in New York, hoping to attract recognition in the nation's center of high fashion?

⟶

Solutions #4: **In Fashion**

A Invest in a small factory, reducing the cost of manufacture by keeping the entire procedure in-house?

▶ **−2 points**   What looks on the surface to be a good way to reduce costs could actually turn out to be counterproductive. The rapid turnover in styles could make it extremely difficult to deal with the manufacturing problems. Additionally, with a luxury item, it is usually not the expense of production that determines success but the acceptance of the product. In a firm such as this, marketing, not production, is the dominant variable. Why take the risks of fluctuating production for marginal gains in cost control?

B Use the capital to expand by setting up additional outlets in other midwestern cities, such as Minneapolis and Omaha?

▶ **3 points**   This is certainly a proven winning strategy, and there is a lot to be said for staying with a successful formula. The fact that there is little in the way of risk is also a strong argument in favor of this approach. This would be the hands-down winner in a climate of recession or with an exceptionally conservative board.

C Establish an outlet in New York, hoping to attract recognition in the nation's center of high fashion?

▶ **5 points**   This is an aggressive move, with a higher reward than any of the other possibilities, but also a higher risk than simply staying in the Midwest. If you bomb in New York, it will probably limit the long-term growth potential of the company. On the other hand, as the song says, "if you can make it there, you'll make it anywhere," and this is especially true in those industries for which New York is a Mecca. Given a solid midwestern base on which to fall back, this is a case in which the potential reward more than justifies the risk.

Score _____   **Running Score for Part I** _____

━━━━━━━━━━━━━━━━━━━━━━━━▶ **THE BOTTOM LINE**

The best time to take a risk is when failure does not lead to catastrophe. All-or-something is a lot more attractive a proposition than all-or-nothing.

Scenario #5

Private Sector

You have just finished a stint with the Department of Commerce, during which you produced a well-received paper entitled "The Role of Flexibility in Maintaining Corporate Profits during Periods of Regulatory Uncertainty." Like so many government employees before you, you have decided to use your government experience as a stepping-stone to the private sector. You have received three equally attractive offers but would obviously like to move into an area that gives you the maximum opportunity to strut your stuff. Should you accept a job with

▶ **A**

A major semiconductor manufacturer that is worried about changes in the regulatory atmosphere concerning Japanese dumping of semiconductors?

or

▶ **B**

A multinational pharmaceutical firm whose American marketing policies are influenced by the ebb and flow at the Food and Drug Administration?

or

▶ **C**

A textile manufacturer that is interested in the probability that increased tariffs will be imposed on foreign imports?

⟶

Solutions #5: **Private Sector**

A A major semiconductor manufacturer that is worried about changes in the regulatory atmosphere concerning Japanese dumping of semiconductors?

▶ **1 point**   There is no question that, if you are able to do a good job of predicting government policy in this area, you will render a major service to your employer, who will know whether to increase or decrease production levels. However, you are putting all your eggs in one basket; namely, can you give a yes or no answer to a critical question? It sounds as if what they really want is a political pundit.

B A multinational pharmaceutical firm whose American marketing policies are influenced by the ebb and flow at the Food and Drug Administration?

▶ **5 points**   Here is a position that seems tailor-made for your capabilities. A multinational pharmaceutical firm has a wide number of inputs and outputs, and tailoring a flexible strategy applicable to a wide range of possibilities should be right up your alley.

C A textile manufacturer that is interested in the probability that increased tariffs will be imposed on foreign imports?

▶ **–1 point**   Obviously, they will be pleased if you tell them that there is a strong probability that tariffs will be increased, but will they shoot the bearer of bad tidings? It sounds as if what they really want is a lobbyist.

Score _____   **Running Score for Part I** _____

━━━━━━━━━━━━━━━━━━━━━━━━━━━━━▶ **THE BOTTOM LINE**

The maximum scope for managerial talent occurs in situations with a multitude of options. With rare exceptions, baseball pitchers with a variety of pitches usually outlast those who depend solely on their fastball.

Scenario #6

Chrome Plated

Chromium is a rare but strategic metal that plays a vital role in the fabrication of various industrial alloys. It is essential for the defense industry, among others, which is why you take some pride in the fact that your chromium import company, which has been doing quite well, plays a constructive role in helping your country. On the other hand, your chief source of supply is South Africa, where you have a long-term contract. Like many Americans, you have become more and more distressed by political conditions in that country, but the fact remains that chromium is where you find it, and much of it is found in South Africa. Your primary duty is to your stockholders, and it is up to you to take steps to make sure that the company's success continues. Is it most important for you to

▶ **A**

Try to work out an arrangement with the South African mining companies to insure that working conditions are adequate so that strikes will not disrupt the mines?

or

▶ **B**

Check for alternative sources of chromium in the world market, in case trade with South Africa is disrupted?

or

▶ **C**

Support an R & D program to find alternative uses for chromium, in case your primary customers find substitutes?

→

Solutions #6: **Chrome Plated**

A Try to work out an arrangement with the South African mining companies to insure that working conditions are adequate so that strikes will not disrupt the mines?

▶ **1 point** It would certainly be constructive if you could make such an arrangement. This would not only be good for your company, it would also add to your image as a humanitarian. However, from the bottom-line standpoint, any strike is liable to be short-lived where the workers have no other means of support, so this is not really a primary concern.

B Check for alternative sources of chromium in the world market, in case trade with South Africa is disrupted?

▶ **3 points** Your business is based on chromium, and without a source of supply you are out of business. In addition, if you can find alternative sources of supply, your position in the chromium import business would strengthen, to say nothing of the fact that you would be able to exert more pressure on your South African connections.

C Support an R & D program to find alternative uses for chromium, in case your primary customers find substitutes?

▶ **5 points** Only one thing can blow you out of the water, and that is for chromium to cease to be of importance. If your primary buyers find substitutes for chromium, it would be imperative for you to find substitutes for your primary buyers, or else a major reversal in your company's fortunes will occur.

Score _____   **Running Score for Part I** _____

━━━━━━━━━━━━━━━━━━━━━━━━━━━━━▶ **THE BOTTOM LINE**

Every business strategy has its primary risk, which must be identified and minimized. If all of your eggs are in one basket, you'd better make sure that there is someone out there who wants to buy eggs.

Scenario #7

Capital Idea

Five years as a short-order cook have not been wasted. You have managed to save a little money, but more importantly, you have perfected the ultimate fast-food french fry, combining a slightly chewy texture and a subtle blend of seasonings to create a superior spud. The world may not beat a path to the door of the builder of a better mousetrap, but it certainly will to the door of the creator of a tastier french fry, or so you believe. However, there is a problem: money. It would take your life savings to go into business for yourself, and there are other possibilities available. Should you

▶ **A**

   Negotiate with the Small Business Administration for a low-interest start-up loan?

   or

▶ **B**

   Take the plunge, withdraw all your savings, and attempt to realize the great American dream?

   or

▶ **C**

   Give in to the imprecations of a well-heeled friend and let him finance the venture for a large piece of the action?

⟶

Solutions #7: **Capital Idea**

A Negotiate with the Small Business Administration for a low-interest start-up loan?

▶ **2 points**   You could do worse. The chief advantage of doing this is that you will not have to start operations on a shoestring. Despite Polonius' advice in *Hamlet* to "neither a borrower nor a lender be," a loan makes sense when there is a pot of gold at the end of the rainbow.

B Take the plunge, withdraw all your savings, and attempt to realize the great American dream?

▶ **1 point**   It worked for Horatio Alger, and it may indeed work for you, but if you have to pinch pennies at every turn, you may find it difficult to succeed. Undercapitalization has killed many a good idea and stunted the growth of countless others.

C Give in to the imprecations of a well-heeled friend, and let him finance the venture for a large piece of the action?

▶ **5 points**   In general, you should be reluctant to give up a piece of the action, but here you are up against the wall, and borrowing money or using your own could have disastrous consequences in case of failure. This way, you will not be devastated if you fail, and you will have half of a large loaf if you succeed. In addition, the probability of success will increase beyond that which could have been expected if you had used only your own funds. It is possible for a gambler to lose all his money on a winning proposition if he or she is betting against a much better-capitalized opponent; this phenomenon is known as Gambler's Ruin and also applies to undercapitalized small businesses.

Score _____   **Running Score for Part I** _____

➡ **THE BOTTOM LINE**

Half of a large loaf is usually better than a small probability of getting an entire loaf. Gamblers who bet the rent money because they think they're on a hot streak soon find themselves out in the cold.

Scenario #8

Tube Steak

Charlie Brown, of the *Peanuts* cartoon strip, once observed, "nothing improves the flavor of a hot dog like putting a ball game in front of it." Be that as it may, you are one of the leading producers of America's favorite beef and pork concoction, and you have nothing to beef about, as America's passion for hot dogs has boosted your profits substantially over the last decade. Nonetheless, it doesn't hurt to keep your eyes peeled for signs of danger, and you have appointed a study group to look for potential trouble areas. Should they investigate

▶ **A**

The possibility that an oriental consortium might buy cheap South American meat, make hot dogs cheaper, and sell them here?

   or

▶ **B**

Alternate sources of supply and ways to hedge the cost, perhaps by using fixed-price contracts or by hedging in the futures market, in anticipation of another drought year, which might cause meat prices to skyrocket?

   or

▶ **C**

Potential trouble on the labor front, as meat-packers feel that their wages have not kept pace with the cost of living?

⟶

Solutions #8: **Tube Steak**

A The possibility that an oriental consortium might buy cheap South American meat, make hot dogs cheaper, and sell them here?

▶ **–1 point**   In all probability, this would be a waste of time. It's certainly possible that this might happen, but it's a somewhat distant threat; in addition, the chances are very strong that an oriental hot dog would taste sufficiently different from an American one as to be unattractive to American taste buds. Marketing foreign foodstuffs is always a problem.

B Alternate sources of supply and ways to hedge the cost, perhaps by using fixed-price contracts or by hedging in the futures market, in anticipation of another drought year, which might cause meat prices to skyrocket?

▶ **5 points**   This is so important that you should be studying the problem at all times. If there are major changes in the price of beef and pork, the price of hot dogs will rise substantially, and you are dealing with consumers who are extremely sensitive to price. You'll still sell them in ballparks, but there will be fewer hot dogs on the dining tables of America.

C Potential trouble on the labor front, as meat-packers feel that their wages have not kept pace with the cost of living?

▶ **2 points**   It's true that you should keep an eye on the problem, because if no hot dogs are produced, you can't sell any. However, it is unlikely that there will be a protracted industry shutdown, and labor is not the chief determinant of the price of hot dogs. Besides, events such as strikes, which occur on an industrywide basis, will affect your competitors as much as they will affect you.

Score _____   **Running Score for Part I** _____

━━━━━━━━━━━━━━━━━━━━━━━━━━━━▶ **THE BOTTOM LINE**

When your strategy is one of low-cost production, you must make every effort to ensure that costs stay low. Eternal vigilance is the price of low-cost leadership.

Scenario #9

Relatively Speaking

It has taken a number of years, but you have created a corporation that runs like a fine watch, with each department autonomous but answerable to the CEO. Suddenly you have a problem: the chief stockholder wants his second cousin to be given a job in management. After a brief but illuminating interview, you realize that this person should be placed in charge of procuring paper clips. It's a tricky situation, made more so by the fact that during a lunch with the chief stockholder, when you tactfully broached your concern, you ran head-on into an attitude of adamant truculence. You've simply GOT to hire the second cousin, and the problem is one of damage control before the damage actually occurs. Should you place this turkey

▶ **A**

In the personnel department, where he can write reports evaluating hiring practices?

or

▶ **B**

In the procurement department, where he can do comparison studies of potential suppliers?

or

▶ **C**

In the sales department, where he can be placed in charge of air conditioner sales in Alaska or something of that ilk?

$\longrightarrow$

Solutions #9: **Relatively Speaking**

A In the personnel department, where he can write reports evaluating hiring practices?

▶ **5 points**   Whenever you are faced with a liability in any sort of business environment, the most important principle is to place it where it will do the least damage. In this instance, the worst that will happen is that the evaluation of hiring practices will be included in the files of the department personnel who actually do the hiring. As long as the departments continue to produce, these reports will have minimal effect.

B In the procurement department, where he can do comparison studies of potential suppliers?

▶ **0 points**   What looks like a perfectly innocuous task can actually boomerang. The world is filled with people who are remarkably short on ability but long on their ability to deceive or sway others. It is perfectly possible that this individual may become convinced that changes should be made in procurement, and through force of personality or proximity to the head honcho influence the opinion of others in the department. It's best not to risk it.

C In the sales department, where he can be placed in charge of air conditioner sales in Alaska or something of that ilk?

▶ **–3 points**   Do not, under any circumstances, place this individual in a position where he can make or sign contracts. If he makes a mistake, it is liable to cost MONEY. Not only will the corporation suffer, but conflicts may arise between you and the chief stockholder.

Score _____   **Running Score for Part I** _____

━━━━━━━━━━━━━━━━━━━━━━━━━━━━▶ **THE BOTTOM LINE**

The more critical the decision, the more important it is that it be made by the most knowledgeable people available. You don't want the inmates running the asylum.

Scenario #10

Ruling the Roost

It's important not to chicken out when it comes to looking for business opportunities, and you certainly wouldn't want to leave any stones unturned when it comes to finding outlets for the poultry grown at your chicken farm. One possibility that has occurred to you is to forward integrate by establishing a chain of chicken restaurants. The bad news is that The Colonel got there first, which obviously puts some sort of an upper limit on the market for new chicken restaurants. On the other hand, at least you know there is a market for chicken; it's possible that fast-food restaurants specializing in octopus might not do so well. You're planning to open a few pilot restaurants; should they be

▶ **A**

Southern-fried chicken restaurants in the tradition of The Colonel, for which there is a huge but possibly saturated market?

   or

▶ **B**

Indian or maybe Italian chicken restaurants, which have yet to make a substantial impact, but which market research indicates may titillate the by-now-jaded palate of the chicken fancier?

   or

▶ **C**

Mexican chicken restaurants, which just started appearing a few years ago, but have caught on and are growing rapidly?

⟶

Solutions #10: **Ruling the Roost**

A Southern-fried chicken restaurants in the tradition of The Colonel, for which there is a huge but possibly saturated market?

▶ **–1 point**   Not on your extra crispy. You might have developed the world's greatest recipe for Southern-fried chicken, but the competition is so fierce that you might have to give it away in order to get people to try it, and then how will you know whether or not you have a winner?

B Indian or maybe Italian chicken restaurants, which have yet to make a substantial impact, but which market research indicates may titillate the by-now-jaded palate of the chicken fancier?

▶ **5 points**   As long as you're simply trying a pilot project, why not go for it? The time to take risks is in the preliminary stage, when the cost of failure is relatively small. If you have a winner, you will be in the enviable position of being a leader in this sector of the market, a leader who can effect cost savings on the supply side. If worst comes to worst, you can take your loss and either try again or simply go back to selling chicken, rather than cooking it as well.

C Mexican chicken restaurants, which just started appearing a few years ago, but have caught on and are growing rapidly?

▶ **3 points**   It certainly doesn't hurt that you are getting into a growing sector of the market, as rapid growth can cover a multitude of sins. Your risk of failure here is less, but the reward for success is not as great in a fragmented market.

Score _____   **Running Score for Part I** _____

➤ **THE BOTTOM LINE**

A good time to take a gamble with a high ratio of reward to risk is when you can afford to lose. Most of the big scores at Las Vegas are made by gamblers going for broke when the fear of losing is not a factor.

Scenario #11

Flaunt It

After years of serving as a highly respected but poorly paid labor negotiator working for the National Labor Relations Board, it's time to sell your services on the open market. Not only do you wish to receive adequate remuneration for your services, but you would also like to have a position in which your skills are on public display, as it has occurred to you that there may well be a place in politics for an individual with your skills as both a negotiator and a communicator. Should you take a job as a negotiator for

▶ **A**

Professional baseball, which would certainly put you on public display, even though the industry itself is peripheral?

or

▶ **B**

Registered nurses, a group of individuals who play a vital role in society and are not treated as well as they deserve?

or

▶ **C**

Air traffic controllers, a small group whose potential power is far out of proportion to their numbers?

→

Solutions #11: **Flaunt It**

A Professional baseball, which would certainly put you on public display, even though the industry itself is peripheral?

▶ **5 points**   From your standpoint, this job has everything going for it. If your services are never used, you will be perceived as having done a good job. If your services are required, it will be on a national basis, and you will be in a highly visible position. Finally, all you have to do is to achieve a settlement; you don't have to WIN for anyone.

B Registered nurses, a group of individuals who play a vital role in society and are not treated as well as they deserve?

▶ **1 point**   The problem here is that nurses' strikes tend to be local rather than national, and so it will be hard for you to achieve a reputation in this area. Additionally, the sympathy of the public is likely to be with the nurses, so you are in a position where you have to win rather than merely achieve a settlement.

C Air traffic controllers, a small group whose potential power is far out of proportion to their numbers?

▶ **-2 points**   Taking this position would leave you in a situation where you have virtually nothing to gain and everything to lose. If things go smoothly, no one will know who you are. If your services are needed, the pressure will be on you to achieve a rapid settlement, not necessarily a fair one. Finally, if you do not achieve a rapid settlement, the government is liable to step in, and you will be seen as having failed.

Score _____   **Running Score for Part I** _____

━━━━━━━━━━━━━━━━━━━━━━▶ **THE BOTTOM LINE**

The same type of planning and decision analysis that is used effectively by organizations should be used by individuals to identify personal goals and choose appropriate actions. If you don't keep your eye on what you want, how do you expect to get it?

Scenario #12

Firepower

Ever since the War of Independence, your small-arms company has done business with the government, supplying American soldiers with rifles and automatic weapons. Your weapons have accompanied Americans from the halls of Montezuma to the shores of Tripoli. Recently, your firm has developed a process that retards heat buildup in the barrel of a gun and is planning to use this process to capture a greater share of the military market for semiautomatic and automatic weapons. You're going to have to tool up to produce prototypes, and you don't want to misuse your potential advantage by firing at the wrong target. Should you

▶ **A**

Manufacture arms that are currently competitive with the industry in overall performance but can be sold for 25 percent less than the going price?

or

▶ **B**

Produce weapons that have the same price and rate-of-fire as the most popular models but twice the stopping power?

or

▶ **C**

Produce weapons that have the same price and stopping power as the most popular models but twice the rate-of-fire?

⟶

Solutions #12: **Firepower**

A Manufacture arms that are currently competitive with the industry in overall performance but which can be sold for 25 percent less than the going price?

▶ **–2 points**   You are in an industry where performance is valued far more than cost, and generating a cost advantage may even be counterproductive. Governments in particular do not wish to equip their troops with the cheapest weapons but with the best. Besides, the taxpayer foots the bill.

B Produce weapons that have the same price and rate-of-fire as the most popular models but have twice the stopping power?

▶ **2 points**   At least you are headed in the right direction with this one. A weapon is valued in proportion to the damage that it can cause, and sheer, raw power is a definite selling point. An additional point here is that your weapon is liable to have a range advantage over others in its class.

C Produce weapons that have the same price and stopping power as the most popular models but have twice the rate-of-fire?

▶ **5 points**   This is the classic dimension by which the effectiveness of weapons is measured. While the additional stopping power might be of some value, the truth is that anyone who gets in the way of a bullet is in trouble, and a higher rate-of-fire increases the probability that the other guy will get hit first.

Score _____   **Running Score for Part I** _____

━━━━━━━━━━━━━━━━━━━━━━━━━━━━▶ **THE BOTTOM LINE**

The most profitable niche in an industry is not always that of the low-cost leader. It's hard to win unless you know what type of game you're playing.

Scenario #13

Pipe Dream

You have been the world's second leading manufacturer of gentlemen's high-quality pipes for more than a century, but the tobacco industry has obviously seen better days. Some of the smaller fry are getting out of the market, and there is a reasonable chance that the leading manufacturer is planning to do so as well. On the other hand, the firm that manufactures your pipe bowls has offered you the choice of either buying their factory directly, which would substantially reduce your costs, or purchasing an option to buy the factory. You wish you had a crystal ball so you could see into the future, as you have no idea what your chief competitor will do. You'd like to get rich, but you don't want to drop a bundle. Should you

▶ **A**

Stick with the status quo and do nothing, planning to resolve the situation when the leader makes its decision?

or

▶ **B**

Purchase an option on the factory and decide what to do when the leader makes its decision?

or

▶ **C**

Purchase the factory, figuring that you will probably buy it anyway, and save the cost of the option?

⟶

Solutions #13: **Pipe Dream**

A Stick with the status quo and do nothing, planning to resolve the situation when the leader makes its decision?

▶ **2 points**   It is fairly obvious that the industries related to tobacco smoking are unlikely to expand rapidly in the near future, and it is possible that you may wish to leave the industry at some time in the not too distant future. On the other hand, if the leader exits, there will be a vacuum that you are in the best position to fill. A wait-and-see attitude that does not risk any capital has something to commend it.

B Purchase an option on the factory and decide what to do when the leader makes its decision?

▶ **5 points**   Options usually cost only a small fraction of the total amount of a purchase, and this could pay *big* dividends if the leader packs it in. You will not only be in a superlative position to capture a large segment of the market, but by exercising the option to buy the factory you will substantially reduce your costs as well, a tremendous double-play combination.

C Purchase the factory, figuring that you will probably buy it anyway, and save the cost of the option?

▶ **0 points**   If the leader leaves the industry, you will be a hero, but all you will have saved will be the price of the option. If the leader sticks around, you will have sunk extra capital into a business with dubious prospects for growth.

Score _____   **Running Score for Part I** _____

━━━━━━━━━━━━━━━━━━━━━━━━━━▶ **THE BOTTOM LINE**

Options provide an excellent way to capitalize on potential good luck without going out on a limb to do so. You pay premiums for both insurance and options; you need insurance to guard against disaster, and options to take advantage of opportunity.

2

An Industry, Its Players, and Their Strategies

THE ISSUES

Industries and Companies

An industry consists of companies that supply products and/or services that can substitute for one another. The boundaries that define industries can sometimes be blurred, as it is possible to think of an airline as a company in both the air travel industry and the transportation industry. If an airline executive were to be asked about the competition, he would probably talk about what the other airlines are doing. In this book, the boundaries will generally be drawn at the level of the air travel industry rather than the transportation industry.

In order to assess both an industry and a company in that industry more accurately, it is important to understand the competitive structure of the industry. That structure depends on the relative strengths and strategies of the competitors, suppliers, and customers, as well as the mobility barriers that exist within the industry. These barriers affect the ease with which newcomers can enter the industry or existing companies can exit the industry without severe costs. The competitive structure also depends on the ease with which companies within the industry can change strategies and compete in another sector of the industry. There may be substantial switching costs required to make such changes.

Industries differ markedly with respect to the relative strength and intensity of competition among participants, as well as the level of mobility barriers and switching costs. These differences exert a powerful force on manufacturing and marketing costs, capital requirements, relative market shares, and prices. Some industry structures allow many companies to earn satisfactory returns over a long time period. In other structures, only a very few firms may be consistently profitable. Often, even well-managed companies have trouble competing successfully. The industry structure, therefore, defines the dominant variables with which a company's strategy must cope.

Basic Strategies for Success in the Industrial Environment

A firm's basic strategy, its rules of action, will determine its fundamental position vis-à-vis its competitors, customers, and suppliers. Firms develop strategies to achieve sustainable advantageous positions in the industry. In defining the basic strategy, the firm must answer two fundamental questions:

1. Does the firm want to compete in a broad market or focus on a limited, perhaps specialized market?
2. Within the chosen market, should the firm strive for low-cost/low-price leadership, or should it differentiate its product to increase its uniqueness and value to customers?

Figure 2.1   Basic Strategic Variables

	Market Focus	
	Broad (B) MARKET	Narrow (N) MARKET
Low-cost (L) PRODUCT	BL	NL
Differentiated (D) PRODUCT	BD	ND

Product Characteristic

These two questions, each with two possible answers, can be treated as two strategic variables: market focus (broad or narrow) and product characteristic (low-cost or differentiated). These two variables give rise to four possible basic strategic choices, which are summarized in Figure 2.1. Any of these four choices, properly executed under the right conditions, can lead to successful long-term performance.

Broad Market Focus, Low-Cost Product (BL)

This strategy aims at overall low-cost leadership. It features low-cost design and large-scale manufacture of a standard product, along with low-cost, wide distribution. There can only be one successful low-cost leader with a broad market focus in an industry.

In order to implement this strategy, the company must utilize efficient, often large-scale operations. Such a strategy gives a company an obvious cost advantage over its competitors, and therefore great negotiating advantages when dealing with potential customers. A competitor will find it difficult to compete head-on with the overall low-cost producer and will usually succeed only by either focusing on a narrow market segment and/or differentiating its product.

Differentiated Product: Broad Market (BD) and Narrow Market (ND)

These two differentiation strategies, one in the broad industry market and the other in a narrow market segment, utilize unique technology, design, reliability, image, or delivery, which enables customers to rationalize a price premium in excess of the costs of differentiation. There may be numerous unique attributes valued by customers, and therefore several successful differentiation strategies can coexist. Thus a company unable to compete directly with the overall low-cost leaders can realize higher profit margins and sustain a competitive position. Differentiated products protect the company from both substitute products and low-cost standard products.

The most significant difference between the broad market (lower left) and narrow market (lower right) choices for the differentiated product lies in the breadth of the appeal of the unique features of the product. Some features, such as unique quality, reliability, or delivery mechanisms, may have universal appeal, so that customers in the broad market would be willing to pay a premium price over that of the low-cost undifferentiated product. On the other hand, highly customized, unique features can be used to satisfy specific needs in narrow market segments. The latter strategy often requires low-volume, high-quality manufacturing where short production runs may be utilized to tailor the product to the customer's specific needs.

Narrow Market Focus, Low-Cost Producer (NL)

This strategy strives for cost leadership in a narrow market segment. It exploits situations where production or marketing costs differ from those of the overall market. The segment may yield a cost advantage to the narrowly focused producer because it doesn't require the same quality or service provided in the broad market. Alternatively, the segment may be so small as to be ignored by the overall low-cost producer, thereby allowing a less efficient producer to attain the lowest cost in the narrow market. Both this strategy and the differentiated narrow market strategy exploit differences in the various market segments. Low-cost production takes advantage of cost differences in these segments, and differentiated production focuses on differences in product or service needs in the various segments. Within a market segment, a firm sustaining cost leadership or product differentiation can be highly profitable. Most industries have numerous market segments providing opportunity for sustainable high performance.

Common Characteristics among the Basic Strategies

Any of these strategies may be viable within a particular industry, although certain characteristics must always be satisfied. The low-cost producer, whether aiming at a broad or narrow market, must be able to do the job efficiently, relying on volume to maintain profitability. The producer focusing on a narrow market segment exploits differences in the various market segments by taking advantage of either cost differences or differences in product or service needs. The producer relying on a differentiation strategy must be able to find a market niche in which there is a demand for a differentiated product.

Strategy, Structure, and Process

The basic *strategy* selected determines the company's identity, including its administrative *structure*, as well as its manufacturing, marketing, and/or servicing *process*. If it attempts to diversify its strategic approach, its structure and process will be less specialized and less efficient, and it will become vulnerable to more focused competitors.

Successfully changing a basic strategy can be a monumental and time-consuming endeavor. Once a strategy is chosen, the company's structure and process must be created specifically to implement that strategy. Lines of authority, levels of responsibility, degrees of decentralization, and logistics must be determined so that the structure can most efficiently implement the strategy. In the same way, manufacturing (job shop, assembly line, automatic, etc.) and other processes, often requiring huge investment, must be designed in a manner congruent with the strategy. Once the structure and process are put in place, they cannot easily or quickly be changed; therefore they become constraints on the adoption of a strategy that is inconsistent with the present structure and process.

If a company has a well-designed and executed strategy, together with a congruent structure and process, it is usually better to seek growth in new industries rather than to accommodate growth by means of a basic strategic change.

Scenario #14

Big Blue

A virtually unbroken string of correct management decisions has landed you the top spot at Colossal Computers, the world leader in business computers, which has had several highly profitable years. The name of the game is growth, and Colossal is now hungrily eyeing the lucrative, but fragmented, personal computer market. The potential in this field has not gone unnoticed, and other firms are scurrying to get in on the action. The R & D division has developed a reasonable PC, and it's time for you to decide whether or not to launch the product. Colossal Computers is certainly a heavyweight, but how heavy a weight should you be willing to throw around? Is the best course of action to

▶ **A**

Get your feet wet by manufacturing and test-marketing the PC in a small number of markets to see what the reaction will be?

or

▶ **B**

Stick to what you do best, namely business computers, and maybe get back into the PC market when the weak sisters have been shaken out?

or

▶ **C**

Go whole hog, throwing the full resources and good name of Colossal Computers behind the product?

→

Solutions #14: **Big Blue**

A Get your feet wet by manufacturing and test-marketing the PC in a small number of markets to see what the reaction will be?

▶ **–2 points**   Test-marketing is a good idea for items that are matters of individual taste, such as beverages, foods, or personal care items. Individual tastes change slowly, but your computer may become obsolete by the time you finish your survey.

B Stick to what you do best, namely business computers, and maybe get back into the PC market when the weak sisters have been shaken out?

▶ **2 points**   There is always something to be said for conservative, disaster-avoiding action, and this decision certainly falls into that category. However, you may regret not having struck while the iron was hot.

C Go whole hog, throwing the full resources and good name of Colossal Computers behind the product?

▶ **5 points**   Here is a terrific opportunity to utilize all the advantages of scale. You have name recognition, an extensive sales force, and large production and research facilities. This gives you an excellent opportunity to seize a significant share of this market. Interestingly enough, both IBM and Digital reached the same conclusion and adopted this strategy, only to end up getting their respective clocks cleaned due to unforeseen developments, such as the rapid growth of the clones. Does this render the decision incorrect? Not at all—it is not the success of individual decisions which is important, but the success of the overall strategy. You may lose a few when you try to utilize your advantages, but in the long run you will come up a winner.

Score _____   **Running Score for Part I** _____

━━━━━━━━━━━━━━━━━━━━━━━▶ **THE BOTTOM LINE**

If you can achieve economies of scale, it is important to take advantage of them. A heavyweight fighter is always dangerous because he can hit so hard.

Scenario #15

Range Finder

You are the head of a division of a large corporation that received what seemed to be a lucrative defense contract to manufacture advanced laser range finders. You retooled and trained your employees, but in the first year of a five-year contract, you only showed a slight profit. Part of the reason is that only 92 percent of the range finders the division produced passed the government guidelines, whereas your profit projection was based on an estimate that 95 percent of the range finders would pass. With one year down and four to go, you have to assess the chances of being able to see whether the light at the end of the tunnel belongs to an onrushing locomotive. Should you

▶ **A**

Purchase new equipment in order to take advantage of improvements in laser manufacturing, which have been made over the last year?

or

▶ **B**

Stand pat, relying on the experience curve to produce the desired improvement in the acceptance rate as your employees become more familiar with the new tools and procedures?

or

▶ **C**

Exercise the cancellation clause in the contract, which would allow you to renege on the remaining four years of the contract without having to show a loss to the higher-ups?

→

Solutions #15: **Range Finder**

A Purchase new equipment in order to take advantage of improvements in laser manufacturing, which have been made over the last year?

▶ **0 points** The trade-off here compares improvements in the manufacturing process with the added expense of purchasing the new equipment and the subsequent retraining. Unless really significant breakthroughs have been made in the field, there is no reason to think that you have horse-and-buggy equipment in the automobile era.

B Stand pat, relying on the experience curve to produce the desired improvement in the acceptance rate as your employees become more familiar with the new tools and procedures?

▶ **5 points** This is the classic environment in which payoffs from the experience curve can be expected. Barring outside catastrophes, you should see significant gains next year.

C Exercise the cancellation clause in the contract, which would allow you to renege on the remaining four years of the contract without having to show a loss to the higher-ups?

▶ **−3 points** It is hard to imagine a scenario under which this would be the right move. A company which expects every single one of its divisions to show substantial profits every single year probably should never accept a long-term contract involving start-up problems in the first place.

Score _____   **Running Score for Part I** _____

━━━━━━━━━━━━━━━━━━━━━━━━▶ **THE BOTTOM LINE**

You make your greatest gains from experience where the learning curve is steepest, and it is almost never so at the outset. A rookie pitcher often blows the opponents off the field the first time through the line-up but gets tagged the next time when they catch on to his or her style.

Scenario # 16

Baggage Check

Luggage manufacturing has been a stable, comfortable industry for the past couple of decades. People will always need luggage, and the major firms are basically content with their price structures, products, and market shares. You're about to change all that, as a project conducted by a division of your conglomerate has managed to devise a way to cut the cost of manufacturing luggage by almost 50 percent, even at low production levels. Traditionally, there are three basic types of luggage, which are roughly equal in total revenue. The infrequent traveler usually goes for inexpensive luggage, the frequent traveler wants durable luggage, and the jet-setter wants high-style luggage. Should you

▶ **A**

Manufacture inexpensive luggage comparable to what's currently on the market and use your process to obtain a clear-cut cost advantage?

or

▶ **B**

Use the money saved by your process to manufacture luggage that can survive anything but an A-bomb, at a price comparable to what's currently on the market?

or

▶ **C**

Use the savings to manufacture high-style luggage that is so individualized that each customer has his or her own pattern?

⟶

Solutions #16: **Baggage Check**

A Manufacture inexpensive luggage comparable to what's currently on the market and use your process to obtain a clear-cut cost advantage?

▶ **5 points** Go for it. In a stable industry with set price structures, you can grab a large share of the market based on price considerations alone. Moreover, the very fact that most members of the industry are currently comfortably ensconced in the status quo should not only slow their reaction time to your move but may prevent them from retaliating at all.

B Use the money saved by your process to manufacture luggage that can survive anything but an A-bomb, at a price comparable to what's currently on the market?

▶ **I point** The major problem here is that, while durability is viewed by many consumers as the key to their purchasing decision, it is not nearly as likely that the marginal gain in durability will cause a customer to change brands the way marginal gains in cost will.

C Use the savings to manufacture high-style luggage that is so individualized that each customer has his or her own pattern?

▶ **2 points** The high end of the market is not price sensitive; therefore, you won't gain a marketing advantage over your competitors with higher costs. Also, the total market is much smaller than the low-cost end.

Score _____   **Running Score for Part I** _____

━━━━━━━━━━━━━━━━━━━━━━━━━━▶ **THE BOTTOM LINE**

In good times or in bad, the low-cost leader in a market is the one who is always assured of a niche. Staying at the bottom can usually keep you on top.

Scenario #17

Heads Up

A window of opportunity has just opened for Headguard Helmets, a manufacturer of helmets for football, hockey, and race car drivers. Over passionate and vocal opposition, the government has just passed a law requiring all motorcyclists to wear helmets or face suspension of their licenses. It is hard not to applaud the government for its sensible stand in this area as you, the head of Headguard, blissfully contemplate greatly increased annual sales and profits. It is a simple matter to adapt any one of your three basic helmet designs to satisfy the government's standards, but you haven't the time or the resources to modify all three. To maximize your profit potential, should you increase production of

▶ **A**

The race car driver's helmet, which comes nearest to the classic motorcycle helmet that is already used by many cyclists?

or

▶ **B**

The football helmet, which offers the most protection, the highest price tag, and the greatest profit per item?

or

▶ **C**

The hockey helmet, which costs the least of the three to manufacture?

──▶

Solutions #17: **Heads Up**

A The race car driver's helmet, which comes nearest to the classic motorcycle helmet that is already used by many cyclists?

▶ **I point**   Because this is similar to the classic motorcycle helmet, there is no question that some of the motorcyclists compelled to buy helmets will choose the classic motorcycle helmet. However, there is a very good chance that, if they choose a classic motorcycle helmet, they will buy it from an established producer of classic motorcycle helmets.

B The football helmet, which offers the most protection, the highest price tag, and the greatest profit per item?

▶ **–2 points**   It's hard to imagine how this decision can come up a winner, unless a bizarre movement springs up to wear football-style helmets to protest the new law. Although these may well be the safest of the three types of helmets, you are not going to be making many sales to customers who are seeking additional safety. If they were seeking additional safety, they would have already purchased a helmet.

C The hockey helmet, which costs the least of the three to manufacture?

▶ **5 points**   An easy winner. Not only is there a built-in advantage in seeking low-cost leadership in a field, but here most of your additional sales will be to people who are being forced to make these purchases and will spend the least amount of money they can in doing so.

Score _____   **Running Score for Part I** _____

━━━━━━━━━━━━━━━━━━━━━━━━▶ **THE BOTTOM LINE**

While there is always a niche for the low-cost leader, the balance tilts even more strongly in that direction when the purchase of an item is mandatory. Given the choice of buying cheap government or good government, which do you think most people would prefer (hint: taxes buy government)?

Scenario #18

Gone Fishing

The bumper sticker on the back of your pickup says, "I'd rather be fishing." That's not surprising, considering that most of the folks around your neck of the woods believe that you have some sort of magical ability when it comes to fishing. It's all nonsense, of course. The truth is that you are the Picasso of dry flies, and it has occurred to you that it should be possible to make a pretty fair living using this ability. You're not asking to get rich, just to make enough to live on, keep the pickup in shape, and give you plenty of time to fish. Should you

▶ **A**

Try to sell your flies to a large chain and have them take care of the merchandising?

or

▶ **B**

Put an ad in magazines such as *Field and Stream,* offering to sell your flies to fishing fanatics?

or

▶ **C**

Just let it be known by word of mouth that you will sell flies, and maybe guide a few charters or similar activity?

⟶

Solutions #18: **Gone Fishing**

A Try to sell your flies to a large chain and have them take care of the merchandising?

▶ **I point** If you have visions of Sears offering your flies throughout the country and giving you a small percentage of every one sold, forget it. Because you cannot single-handedly supply enough for Sears, they would have to be mass-produced. Once the designs are known, they don't need YOU. In order to merchandise something in volume, you either have to handle the manufacturing, financing, or distribution. If you can't do that, you've got to know somebody who will. Do you? It sure doesn't sound like it.

B Put an ad in magazines such as *Field and Stream,* offering to sell your flies to fishing fanatics?

▶ **–I point** You would have to dip into your own pocket to pay for an ad in a magazine, and how will you differentiate your product? It will be hard to convince the typical reader that your flies are any better than others in the same magazine. Save your money.

C Just let it be known via word of mouth that you will sell your flies, and maybe guide a few charters or similar activity?

▶ **5 points** By far your best bet, as it certainly sounds like folks will probably take you up faster than a hungry trout can strike at one of your flies. It's important to be able to offer such extras as personal service when competing for a particular market sector, and you are well placed to do just that. Product uniqueness, service, and custom design reputation are your strengths, and this option capitalizes on all of them.

Score _____   **Running Score for Part I** _____

━━━━━━━━━━━━━━━━━━━━━━━━━━▶ **THE BOTTOM LINE**

Focusing on a particular sector of the market is a viable strategy and must be examined when the alternatives, low-cost leadership and product differentiation, are unattractive or impossible. If you don't have access to a rapid-fire weapon, you are much more likely to bring down a target if you are an accurate shot.

Scenario #19

Ship Shape

After a life spent as a boat bum and five years working for a major boat builder, watching the industry grow as more and more people realize the pleasures to be gained on the world's lakes and oceans, you and a few friends have accumulated enough capital to get started in the business yourself. At the outset, however, you cannot design and build a complete product line, so you have to pick one particular type of vessel, design it, and build it. This is the make-or-break decision for your company; if you make the wrong choice, you'll probably go belly-up. Should you design and build

▶ **A**

Small boats, to take advantage of the expanding market and make your profit on volume?

or

▶ **B**

Fishing boats, which are larger but have a larger profit per vessel?

or

▶ **C**

Custom-built boats, of which you will be able to build only a few at the outset?

$\longrightarrow$

Solutions #19: **Ship Shape**

A Small boats, to take advantage of the expanding market and make your profit on volume?

▶ **–2 points**   Instead of sailing happily off into the sunset, you are more likely to find yourself drowning in a sea of red ink. The mass market for low-cost boats will be won by those manufacturers who can introduce economies of scale. No matter how hard you try, you will not be able to build a small boat at competitive prices, and you'll be sunk before you start.

B Fishing boats, which are larger but have a larger profit per vessel?

▶ **0 points**   At least you've got a chance here, since the larger margins you will need to show a profit can be more readily absorbed by a larger product. However, you still have to sell these boats, and it's going to be hard to find a market. It may even be hard to let your potential customers know that you have a product they might be able to use.

C Custom-built boats, of which you will be able to build only a few at the outset?

▶ **5 points**   At the start, this is precisely what you want to do. When a boat is custom-built, you have an immediate market for your product, and you don't have to worry about selling it. In addition, you will be able to price your product to compensate for the higher cost of materials and manufacturing that you, as a small-scale producer, are forced to incur. Later on, when you have developed a reputation, and perhaps have also built a particularly desirable model, you can consider the possibility of entering a wider market.

Score _____   **Running Score for Part I** _____

━━━━━━━━━━━━━━━━━━━━━━━━━━▶ **THE BOTTOM LINE**

It is important to pay attention to ways to circumvent or minimize entry barriers, which are usually highest to those competitors aiming at low-cost leadership. When starting a small business, dream big, but think small.

3

Competitive Actions and Market Signals

THE ISSUES

Competition is one of the chief driving forces behind the free market system and is perhaps the main reason why market-based economies are more successful than externally regulated ones. Competitive forces work not only to benefit the customer, guaranteeing a wider choice of fairly priced goods and services, but they also work to the advantage of the business that knows how to utilize them.

Sustaining and improving the firm's long-term competitive position requires investment in both defensive and offensive strategies, as well as analyzing what competitors are saying and doing.

Defensive Strategies

Defensive actions are calculated to reduce the probability of, and the vulnerability to, destructive attack by both current competitors and new entrants. A company using a low-cost strategy has a structural barrier against challenge, especially if the low-cost position is the result of production or marketing economies of scale. The challenger could not seriously threaten until it achieved such economies; it would be at a relative cost disadvantage. Other barriers such as product differentiation, favorable relationships with distributors and suppliers, as well as high customer switching costs, may also deter challengers. However, existing barriers and competitor motivations must be understood because challengers will attempt to break down or circumvent these obstacles.

The threat of significant retaliation can increase the perceived cost to the challenger and thereby reduce the probability of challenge, especially if the expectation is for massive and immediate retaliation. The defending firm must give clear and convincing signals demonstrating that its defensive actions will be effective and long lasting.

The probability of a destructive attack can also be reduced by lowering the payoff associated with a successful challenge. If the defending firm reduces its profits, by lowering prices or providing more service, the challenging firm will have less motivation to invade the market. The defensive actions chosen should be those that are effective against the specific attackers most likely to challenge the firm's position.

Offensive Strategies

A successful offense must be designed to overcome the defensive strategies described above, which can be executed by a successful, well-entrenched company willing and able to retaliate. Offensive strategies can therefore be risky, especially a direct assault that imitates the basic strategy of the defender in the same market sector. Such a challenge is extremely costly and seldom successful.

A successful challenge requires that the challenger create either a low-cost or a differentiation advantage over the defender. Customers must perceive *both* a competitive cost and value. Even if the challenger possesses a favorable competitive position, a high probability of success requires some assurance that the defender will not retaliate on such a scale as to make the costs unacceptable to the challenger. The potential challenger must thoroughly analyze the defender's strategies, motivations, and plans.

Market Signals

In analyzing the competitive aspect of a company's actions, there are two factors that must be examined: what are the various competitors *saying* and what are they *doing*. Although actions generally speak louder than words, the words chosen often give valuable clues to the future actions of the competitors. A company performing a competitive analysis must never forget that it, too, is one of the competitors. Other ears will be listening to what *it* says, and other eyes will be watching what *it* does.

By analyzing competitors' motivations, capabilities, and actions, their strengths and weaknesses can be assessed. This will enable the observer to make reasonable predictions about their probable moves, whether these moves be offensive, defensive, or retaliatory in nature.

Just as a competitor's actions give valuable market information to a firm, the firm can communicate its own intentions by signals. These market signals may take the form of announced intentions, price changes, warnings, or bluffs. Like actions, these signals can be offensive, defensive, conciliatory, or retaliatory.

The environment in an industry is similar to the environment that exists in the international political arena. Both business and global politics are games and are therefore amenable to analyses such as those made in game theory. The more complex the game, the wider the scope for both successful and unsuccessful moves. Sometimes the successful moves will be competitive in nature. These moves might increase market share directly, through such tactics as lowering prices. Other moves may increase market share indirectly, perhaps by denying a competitor access to critical information or crucial supplies.

But actions will be taken sequentially, and any contemplated move that threatens competitors must take into account the reactions of those competitors. The likelihood and probable effectiveness of retaliation must be assessed before the move is made. Such assessment sometimes shows that nonthreatening or even cooperative moves will result in better long-term payoffs.

It is an irrefutable fact that, within an industry, firms are affected by, and will react to, competitive moves by others. Therefore, it is important to assess and even try to influence the reaction of other firms. Often a nondestructive reaction can be encouraged if the firm's competitive moves are calculated to further the interests of the industry as a whole rather than the narrow interest of the firm.

Scenario #20

In the Chips

You are the CEO of Emerging Electronics, a company that has already established a comfortable niche producing top-of-the-line products. Your R & D division has been hard at work looking at various possibilities and is fairly certain that it can produce dynamic random-access memory chips at a market price of $4. The good news is that Megabyte Memories, the industry low-cost leader in producing these chips, has already announced that it will produce them at a market price of $5. The bad news is that, if push comes to shove, you are reasonably sure Megabyte can market them at $3, making a small but substantially reduced profit because of Megabyte's large volume. You'd like to maintain a chance to end up in the chips if possible but would like to avoid a major disaster that would have a deleterious effect on your company's performance. Should you

▶ **A**

Tell your R & D manager to look at something else?

or

▶ **B**

Go into production, planning to sandbag Megabyte Memories with a lower price when you both bring the chips to market?

or

▶ **C**

Announce your plans to manufacture and sell the chips at $4, forcing Megabyte to fish or cut bait?

→

Solutions #20: **In the Chips**

A Tell your R & D manager to look at something else?

▶ **2 points**   It's likely that Megabyte will seek to retain control of the market, so it's a reasonably safe bet that you will never go into production. This is also consistent with your firm's basic strategy of manufacturing top-of-the-line products.

B Go into production, planning to sandbag Megabyte Memories with a lower price when you both bring the chips to market?

▶ **–3 points**   This is the type of move that is liable to have stockholders screaming for blood. Yours. Even though you might do quite well if you can market the chips at $4, the odds are very high that Megabyte will act to protect its position, and you cannot afford to invite retaliation from the low-cost leader.

C Announce your plans to manufacture and sell the chips at $4, forcing Megabyte to fish or cut bait?

▶ **5 points**   There is an outside possibility that Megabyte wants out of this particular segment of the market, and by formulating this test of competitor sentiment you might well get an opportunity to step in. If Megabyte announces that they will sell the chips for $3, you can retire gracefully without having committed any capital. Making this announcement also has the advantage of avoiding costly simultaneous moves. Although it would be a disaster if Megabyte makes no announcement, produces its chips, and then brings them to market at $3, thereby making you eat your investment, Megabyte may be unlikely to risk your already having landed a bunch of contracts for $4 chips.

Score _____   **Running Score for Part I** _____

━━━━━━━━━━━━━━━━━━━━━━━━━━━━▶ **THE BOTTOM LINE**

It is always advisable to find out the intentions of the low-cost leader if this can be done without making a financial commitment. The best time to challenge a stronger opponent is when he or she has said he or she is unwilling to fight.

Scenario #21
Soft Touch

Despite the fact that your firm's only product, a powdered fabric softener, is packaged in an unattractive battleship-gray box and has been aiming its advertising at the wrong demographic group, you are showing adequate profits. Adequate is not good enough, and you are considering steps to improve your bottom line. Your product is priced competitively with the fabric softeners marketed by the two companies who are the industry giants, and a survey shows that if you reduce your price to just above your break-even point, the increased volume will enable you to increase your profits. Should you

▶ **A**

Go along with what everyone else is doing and package your fabric softener in a brightly colored box with a floral display?

or

▶ **B**

Retarget your advertising to reflect the changing demographics of fabric softener consumers?

or

▶ **C**

Lower your price to gain a clear-cut price advantage on your primary competitors?

⟶

Solutions #21: **Soft Touch**

A Go along with what everyone else is doing and package your fabric softener in a brightly colored box with a floral display?

▶ **0 points**   Just because your battleship-gray box sticks out like a sore thumb is no reason to reject it. In fact, your buyers probably have no difficulty identifying it among all the other brightly colored containers. If you change the packaging, you are spending money to confuse your loyal clientele.

B Retarget your advertising to reflect the changing demographics of fabric softener consumers?

▶ **5 points**   This is clearly your best shot. Changing the advertising, perhaps even emphasizing your 'battleship-gray' box to increase the differentiation factor, is unlikely to adversely affect your current customers. If they're satisfied, they'll continue to use it. You may be able to persuade enough in the targeted group to give your product a try so as to generate a healthy increase in sales. Equally important, your chief competitors are not as likely to react violently to your change in strategy.

C Lower your price to gain a clear-cut price advantage on your primary competitors?

▶ **–2 points**   This is a move that is loaded with potential hazards. Even if it works initially, when the major players see what you have done and its impact on them, they are likely to retaliate. The result will be a price war in which you are the most likely loser because the big guys can not only dish it out, they can take it and take it longer and harder than you can.

Score _____   **Running Score for Part I** _____

━━━━━━━━━━━━━━━━━━━━━━━━━━━━➤ **THE BOTTOM LINE**

It is almost never advisable to launch a frontal, price-lowering attack on a stronger, better capitalized company. One of the classic lessons of the twentieth century is that guerilla warfare often succeeds where all-out blitzes fail.

Scenario #22

Hot Item

Your electronic components factory has been happily manufacturing standardized parts for electrical appliances for years: motors, heating elements, and the like. Your firm is doing as well as could be expected, without the slightest thought of becoming a Fortune 500 company, when some of your engineers develop a process that can manufacture entire microwave ovens at a substantial savings. This is a potentially profitable development, but one trip to an appliance store will convince you that practically everyone manufactures microwave ovens. Nonetheless, there just HAS to be a way to make money from this. Does your best chance lie in

▶ **A**

Patenting the process and selling it outright to the highest bidder?

or

▶ **B**

Spinning off a microwave oven subsidiary, hoping to capture the substantial low-cost segment of the market?

or

▶ **C**

Contracting with one of the major electrical appliance firms to produce your microwave ovens under their label?

➡

Solutions #22: **Hot Item**

A Patenting the process and selling it outright to the highest bidder?
▶ **I point**   This is certainly a good way to show an extra profit for the coming fiscal year and avoid unnecessary complications. On the other hand, just washing your hands of the entire affair certainly will not move you out of the minor leagues, where your company is currently mired.

B Spinning off a microwave oven subsidiary, hoping to capture the substantial low-cost segment of the market?
▶ **–2 points**   If there were only a few microwave manufacturers, this could well be the right move. However, the market is highly competitive, you are departing from what you do best, and this is a risky maneuver, which will probably amount to biting off more than you can chew. What will you do about distribution channels and advertising, for instance? These will certainly make your oven cost more than you had planned.

C Contracting with one of the major electrical appliance firms to produce your microwave ovens under their label?
▶ **5 points**   This is almost certainly your best shot. If you can arrange such a deal, you will have an opportunity to grow simply because you will be producing large quantities for a major player. In addition, such an alliance could prove fruitful in other ways. If you do well on this project, you may find yourself becoming a major subcontractor somewhere down the line.

Score _____   **Running Score for Part I** _____

━━━━━━━━━━━━━━━━━━━━━━━━━━▶ **THE BOTTOM LINE**

A profitable alliance with an industry leader is often an excellent way to improve a company's performance. You are less likely to be picked on by the neighborhood bully if you have a big brother or sister to watch out for you.

Scenario #23

Classic Vintage

A scandal has recently taken place in France. The major exporter of top-of-the-line French wines has been shipping a rather pretentious *vin ordinaire* to the United States under a vintage label. As an importer of vintage wines, you are torn between rejoicing at the fiasco that has hit your chief competitor and deploring the effect that this has had on the vintage wine business in general. Surveys show that people are actually switching to (Horrors!) domestic wines, running the risk of permanent damage to their palates. How can you best show a profit in the short run without risking disaster in the long run? Should you

▶ **A**

Rush to claim leadership in imported vintages by stressing the reliability of your product and casting doubt by inference on the reliability of your chief rival's?

or

▶ **B**

Conduct a campaign emphasizing the taste, distinction, and breeding associated with vintage wines?

or

▶ **C**

Ignore the whole thing, relying on the fact that the public has a short memory; in the meantime you will make hay as connoisseurs switch to your product in droves?

→

Solutions #23: **Classic Vintage**

A Rush to claim leadership in imported vintages by stressing the reliability of your product and casting doubt by inference on the reliability of your chief rival's?

▶ **–1 point**   You might conceivably be cutting off your nose to spite your face here. It is rarely good practice to bring up reminders of events that tarnish your industry as a whole, and pointing fingers at the perpetrators leaves residual bitterness that might cause your chief rival to look for ways to retaliate if and when the shoe is on the other foot.

B Conduct a campaign emphasizing the taste, distinction, and breeding associated with vintage wines?

▶ **5 points**   You don't have to worry about your market share, at least in the short term. What you have to worry about is the effects of a long-term black eye for the entire industry. Connoisseurs may flock to you not only for the quality of your wines, but in appreciation of what you are doing for the industry as a whole. In addition, scoring brownie points with your competitor in their hour of need may turn out to be bread cast upon the waters.

C Ignore the whole thing, relying on the fact that the public has a short memory; in the meantime you will make hay as connoisseurs switch to your product in droves?

▶ **1 point**   The odds are that this scandal will indeed pass, but in the meantime you want to do what you can in the way of damage control; it certainly won't hurt to earn the gratitude of your competitors with a statesmanlike stance.

Score _____   **Running Score for Part I** _____

══════════════════════════════════▶ **THE BOTTOM LINE**

Too often the rush for short-term profits overlooks potential long-term damage. It is far better to try to repair a leaky ship than to try to become the captain.

Scenario #24

Platter Pilots

Last year's performance of your chain of Top 40 radio stations has not been music to your ears. True, you've seen these cycles before, but the kickback scandal in the industry didn't help matters. A survey was taken, which showed that teenagers were ignoring your stations to do their homework! A bunch of locally owned and operated Top 40 stations have gone on the market recently, and you are considering taking advantage of the soft market to expand. The prices certainly seem favorable, but your chief competitors, the other two major Top 40 chains, seem strangely reluctant to gobble them up. They're practically yours for the taking. Should you

▶ **A**

Trust your instincts and experience and take advantage of those low prices to buy up other stations?

or

▶ **B**

Follow the same basic game plan as the other two major chains and adopt a wait-and-see attitude?

or

▶ **C**

Pull in your own horns and put some of your poorer-producing stations on the market?

⟶

Solutions #24: **Platter Pilots**

A Trust your instincts and experience and take advantage of those low prices to buy up other stations?

▶ **3 points**   This is probably not a bad move, especially since you've seen the market go soft before. Prices always fluctuate, but your expansion plans and familiarity with the market give you an excellent chance to improve the value of these assets beyond what the market currently believes they are worth. If you buy now, the odds are that the prices will go up eventually. Also, the station licenses always have some value, which will reduce your downside risk.

B Follow the same basic game plan as the other two major chains and adopt a wait-and-see attitude?

▶ **5 points**   The two other large chains did not claw their way to the top of the heap of a highly competitive business by making a lot of dumb moves. They're not buying because they probably expect prices to get even softer. When BOTH chains stay out of the market, it looks like they know something you don't. Inaction by respected competitors can often be a market signal and should not be ignored.

C Pull in your own horns and put some of your poorer-producing stations on the market?

▶ **−2 points**   To do this is somewhat akin to trying to extinguish a fire by pouring gasoline on it. By putting some of your own stations on the market, you will depress prices further and maybe trigger similar behavior in the other large chains. As long as you believe that the industry as a whole is still healthy, there is no cause for panic.

Score _____   **Running Score for Part I** _____

━━━━━━━━━━━━━━━━━━━━━━━━━▶ **THE BOTTOM LINE**

It's fine to have faith in your own judgment, but one should never ignore what the competitors in a market environment are doing. If you can keep your head while all around you are losing theirs, maybe you don't understand the situation.

Scenario #25

Soup's On

The souperpower rivalry is heating up. No, it's not a misprint; you and your chief competitor control 64 percent of the highly lucrative multibillion-dollar international soup market. An uneasy truce has preserved the balance of power over the last decade, but suddenly your rival has signaled its aggressive tendencies by launching a lowered-price attack against one of your chief strongholds, cream-style soups. You don't want to escalate hostilities to the point where a nuclear winter scenario might devastate both your profit pictures, but it's important to let them know you have no intention of being pushed around. Should you respond by

▶ **A**

Lowering the price of your cream-style soups in order to retake your traditional share of this important market sector?

or

▶ **B**

Attempting to perpetrate an intelligence coup by luring one of their executives into your camp at a substantial increase in salary if he or she will divulge your rival's battle plans?

or

▶ **C**

Instigating a measured response by launching an initiative of your own against their stronghold: dry soups?

──▶

Solutions #25: **Soup's On**

A Lowering the price of your cream-style soups in order to retake your traditional share of this important market sector?

▶ **1 point** This limited-war scenario has two basic disadvantages. First, your rival may decide to continue the cream-style soup battle, and you could suffer heavy losses because of your substantial market share. In addition, you have signaled your intention to meet force with force, and your competitor may react by expanding the conflict to other areas.

B Attempting to perpetrate an intelligence coup by luring one of their executives into your camp at a substantial increase in salary if he or she will divulge your rival's battle plans?

▶ **−2 points** This could have potentially devastating consequences. Knowledge of your rival's plans would undoubtedly give you a strong temporary advantage, but the resulting shake-up might create a chaotic situation which would hurt both of you. Worse yet, once the leak is discovered they might change plans, and you will have paid a fortune for yesterday's newspaper.

C Instigating a measured response by launching an initiative of your own against their stronghold: dry soups?

▶ **5 points** Countering obliquely by attacking in another area lets your rival know that you won't be bullied, but are willing to let matters subside. When you both have substantial shares of markets, it is also a very good strategic move to lower the price in a market where your competitor's market share is larger, as he or she has more to lose than you do. Such a move will hit him or her where it hurts—in the bottom line.

Score _____   **Running Score for Part I** _____

━━━━━━━━━━━━━━━━━━━━━━━━━▶ **THE BOTTOM LINE**

Countering an attack in one area with an attack in another demonstrates both your strength and your intention not to let things get out of hand. There are times when counterpunching may be a lot more effective than slugging it out toe-to-toe.

Scenario #26

Food Fight

For years, you and your primary competitor have been waging a hotly contested battle in regional foods; maple sugar and codfish cakes in New England, hush puppies and hominy grits in the South, and Tex–Mex in the Sun Belt. Last year, your rival announced that it was pursuing a "Southern Strategy," sinking large sums into advertising and promotions south of the Mason–Dixon line. Though badly outmanned, your troops fought bravely but to no avail, and it is now painfully clear that, although your southern operations are still marginally profitable, your rival has succeeded. Business goes on, though, and it's up to you to formulate a new plan of action. Should you

▶ **A**

Abandon the South entirely and concentrate on improving your profit margins in other areas of the country?

or

▶ **B**

Concentrate your efforts on the other areas of the country but still maintain a presence in the South?

or

▶ **C**

Try to retake the profitable South by countering with increased advertising and promotions of your own?

$\longrightarrow$

Solutions #26: **Food Fight**

A Abandon the South entirely and concentrate on improving your profit margins in other areas of the country?

▶ **0 points**   You may have lost the battle, but you certainly haven't lost the war. If you were showing substantial losses in the South, this would undoubtedly be a course of action worth considering. As things stand, though, abandoning the field would free your competitor from your potential threat to it and allow it to easily put pressure on you in other areas without the threat of oblique counterattack.

B Concentrate your efforts on the other areas of the country but still maintain a presence in the South?

▶ **5 points**   Seeing that your rival has devoted a large portion of its resources to this region, its defenses are undoubtedly thin elsewhere, and now is the time to locate and strike by cross-parrying at the soft underbelly of its position. It is important to maintain a position in the South, so that you can capitalize in case of a slipup, and also to maintain the threat of retaliation in an area where it is strong.

C Try to retake the profitable South by countering with increased advertising and promotions of your own?

▶ **−2 points**   There's a saying in poker that it is unwise to throw good money after bad, and this would be a clear instance of doing so. It certainly isn't clear that your attempt to regain the South would be successful, and even if it were, it might provoke your competitor into a costly price war, which could severely hurt both of you. It has clearly signaled its intention to engage in all-out combat in that region.

Score _____   **Running Score for Part I** _____

━━━━━━━━━━━━━━━━━━━━━━━━━━━━▶ **THE BOTTOM LINE**

When a competitor concentrates resources in one area, there is almost certainly some area that will be left vulnerable. Grow and expand where your opponent is weak, but be prepared to retaliate where it is strong.

Scenario #27

Playing Ketchup

Tomatoes are your business, your only business, and you have just managed to produce a ketchup that is the equal of the market leader in thickness and flavor but for a substantially lower cost. Your competitor's ketchup is the flagship of his or her product line and has the lion's share of the ketchup market. However, tomatoes are only a small part of your rival's business, whereas they're all you've got. You'd hate to sink a lot of money into ketchup production and end up in a price war with the leader, but there must be a way to make some money on this without your rival making hamburger of you. Should you

▶ **A**

Avoid competing directly for "mainline" ketchup sales and aim at a special niche (perhaps very upscale or pitched at a certain group), then use the low cost to give bigger markups to retailers?

or

▶ **B**

Bring it into the national market, but price it only a little below your competitor's?

or

▶ **C**

Bring it into the national market at its low price, which will generate your largest profits?

➡️

Solutions #27: **Playing Ketchup**

A Avoid competing directly for "mainline" ketchup sales and aim at a special niche (perhaps very upscale or pitched at a certain group), then use the low cost to give bigger markups to retailers?

▶ **5 points**   It's best to settle for the proverbial half a loaf. You must send market signals which minimize provocation so that your rival realizes that you are merely trying to carve out a small niche for yourself. Tread carefully here, because if you get too big for your britches, your competitor can conduct a localized price war without placing his or her profit picture in much jeopardy. You are vulnerable because, for you, tomatoes are the whole enchilada, whereas they're just nachos to him or her.

B Bring it into the national market, but price it only a little below your competitor's?

▶ **I point**   Your competitor may well feel that the marginal gain from saving a few pennies is unlikely to dissuade the majority of his or her loyal customers. However, if your sales do very well, you'd better prepare for war. You'd almost rather your sales did okay rather than very well.

C Bring it into the national market at its low price, which will generate your largest profits?

▶ **–2 points**   This has about as much chance as Finland would have if it invaded Russia. Your best chance of achieving your goals is for your competitor to ignore you, and here you are challenging him or her to come out and fight. If you really antagonize him or her, he or she might try to extend the battlefront beyond ketchup, with potentially disastrous consequences for you.

Score _____   **Running Score for Part I** _____

━━━━━━━━━━━━━━━━━━━━━━━━━━➤ **THE BOTTOM LINE**

It rarely pays to provoke a strong competitor to retaliate. A lion might kill another animal that challenges it over a carcass, yet leave plenty of scraps for the scavengers.

Scenario #28

Image Problem

As the leader in the field of children's toys, you suddenly find your-self confronted by a rather unusual problem. Horrortoys, one of your smaller rivals, recently put out a product line of toys that gives new meaning to the phrase 'bad taste,' and both parent-teacher groups and the media are sounding the battle cry. These particular toys are actually doing quite well, but the image of the toy industry and, more importantly, its overall sales are suffering. Something has to be done and soon, as other firms are considering tooling up to produce more of the same. Should you

▶ **A**

Figure that if you can't lick 'em, join 'em, and rush in with a similar line of toys to claim your share of this potentially ex-panding market?

or

▶ **B**

Let it be known throughout the industry that this is having a bad effect, and that if the toys are not taken off the market, you will enter Horrortoys' general market niche, underprice everyone, and devastate Horrortoys' long-term profit picture?

or

▶ **C**

Decide that this is only a temporary trend, ignore the horror market, and launch a "Mr. Clean" marketing campaign to play up the fun and educational value of your own toys?

⟶

Solutions #28: **Image Problem**

A Figure that if you can't lick 'em, join 'em, and rush in with a similar line of toys to claim your share of this potentially expanding market?

▶ **–3 points**   Under no circumstances should you do this, as you would be biting off your nose to spite your face. This is a classic case of trying to win the battle, but losing the war. Because you are the industry leader, it is the overall picture that is of most concern to you.

B Let it be known throughout the industry that this is having a bad effect, and that if the toys are not taken off the market, you will enter Horrortoys' general market niche, underprice everyone, and devastate Horrortoys' long-term profit picture?

▶ **–2 points**   At first sight, it is very appealing to walk softly but carry a big stick. Your threat as an industry leader will be taken seriously, especially if you have gained credibility by acting in the past as you have announced you would. A small rival shouldn't risk angering the powers that be. However, this is a no-win decision. Your public image will take a tumble if you are forced to carry out this threat, but if you don't carry out this threat you will lose credibility.

C Decide that this is only a temporary trend, ignore the horror market, and launch a "Mr. Clean" marketing campaign to play up the fun and educational value of your own toys?

▶ **5 points**   Certain toys are faddish in nature, and these will probably go the way of Hula Hoops and Rubik Cubes. It would be unwise to establish a policy of overreacting by retaliating at the drop of a hat. It is probably more consistent with your company's long-term goals for you to take advantage of the adverse public and media reaction through constructive behavior.

Score _____   **Running Score for Part I** _____

━━━━━━━━━━━━━━━━━━━━━━▶ **THE BOTTOM LINE**

If it will greatly damage you to carry out a threat, you probably shouldn't have made it in the first place. In a mudslinging contest, the one wearing the nicest clothes has the most to lose.

Scenario #29

Deep Thinking

There is no question that artificial intelligence is going to be one of the most important developments in the computer game. As one of the leading software developers, you were in on the ground floor, which unfortunately seems to have crumbled under you. Your heavy investment in R & D and new technology has reaped some rewards, but the technology is currently faced with the threat of becoming obsolete. Despite the fact that you are still in the lead in this area, there is severe danger that you may be nosed out at the wire by firms that enter the game now, utilizing your advances and the newer technology. While that wouldn't be fatal, you'd like to maintain your leadership while effecting as much of a savings as possible. Should you

▶ **A**

Announce that you have made the critical breakthroughs and will be going into production relatively soon?

or

▶ **B**

Announce that the critical breakthroughs are still years away, possibly deterring others from entering the field, and gradually phase in the new technology?

or

▶ **C**

Postpone any announcement, load up on the new technology, and rely on your experience to keep you in the lead?

⟶

Solutions #29: **Deep Thinking**

A Announce that you have made the critical breakthroughs and will be going into production relatively soon?

▶ **0 points**   Bluffing is often a valuable weapon, but this particular bluff is ill-advised. While you might keep some potential players out of the game, others will go in, sensing that the moment of birth is at hand. If you fail to produce quickly, you run the risk of damaging your credibility later.

B Announce that you believe the critical breakthroughs are still years away, possibly deterring others from entering the field, and gradually phase in the new technology?

▶ **3 points**   This bluff has a reasonable chance of accomplishing your goals without damaging your credibility. One of the advantages of running this particular bluff is that you can see how the industry reacts. If your bluff is called, well, rapid progress is always welcome, even if you were unable to foresee it.

C Postpone any announcement, load up on the new technology, and rely on your experience to keep you in the lead?

▶ **5 points**   The odds are that at some stage you are going to have to load up on the technology anyway. The bullet will have to be bitten, so why delay the inevitable? Your added experience has put you higher up on the learning curve, and that will certainly give you some sort of advantage, which will partially offset the investment you made in premature technology. When a "prospector" firm, one which chooses a fundamental strategy of finding new markets and creating new products, succeeds, it profits heavily from its successes. As others enter the field, it must continually make new breakthroughs, or it will decline rapidly.

Score _____   **Running Score for Part I** _____

━━━━━━━━━━━━━━━━━━━━▶ **THE BOTTOM LINE**

It is senseless to bluff if there is no chance that the bluff will be taken seriously. Good poker players know that bluffs can often win small pots and sometimes win medium-sized ones but almost never win big ones.

Scenario #30

Growing Concern

You can't have too mulch of a good thing, and that's especially true of It's Just Too Mulch, the country's largest and fastest-growing manufacturer of garden goods, of which you are the head. Not only is growing your business, but your business is growing; more and more people are going back to nature and getting into gardening. Things are going so well that you are going to build a new factory to manufacture even more mulch. However, a sack of mulch sitting on the shelf is simply a sack of you-know-what if you can't sell it, and you want to expand without triggering a frenzy of expansion by others. Should you

▶ **A**

Announce your intentions in advance, while adding that overexpansion would weed out many of the marginal firms; then go ahead and expand immediately?

or

▶ **B**

Go ahead and expand; you'll be there firstest with the mostest, and the others will drop by the wayside?

or

▶ **C**

Hold off on expansion until you are sure that the industry demand will continue to expand well into the future?

⟶

Solutions #30: **Growing Concern**

A Announce your intentions in advance, while adding that overexpansion would weed out many of the marginal firms; then go ahead and expand immediately?

▶ **5 points**   This is your best bet to have your cake and eat it, too. You have made the decision to expand. Your announcement will deter some others from doing the same or at least force a delay in doing so, and overcapacity will be less of a risk. In addition, your announcement plus your follow-up action will enhance your future credibility.

B Go ahead and expand; you'll be there firstest with the mostest, and the others will drop by the wayside?

▶ **2 points**   Napoleon once said that God is on the side of the heavy battalions, and industry leaders usually stay industry leaders unless they make a major mistake. If you have correctly assessed the situation, expansion of demand will probably assure your additional profits, but you are liable to find that the industry as a whole will add capacity as well, thereby increasing the chance of industry overcapacity and the inherent price cutting that follows.

C Hold off on expansion until you are sure that the industry demand will continue to expand well into the future?

▶ **–1 point**   Failure to expand now is acting like a poker player who refuses to bet until he holds a sure thing. Commerce is a game of risk and reward, and unless you take intelligently planned risks, you will end up minimizing your rewards. Admittedly, there are certainly times when it is right to wait, but failing to add capacity when you are the industry leader in an expanding environment is the height of cowardice.

Score _____   **Running Score for Part I** _____

━━━━━━━━━━━━━━━━━━━━━━━━━━━━▶ **THE BOTTOM LINE**

Credible announcements of intentions to expand, especially by the industry leader, can reduce the likelihood of overexpansion. If you want people to stay out of the kitchen, turn up the heat.

Scenario #31

A Pizza the Action

Your monthly spreadsheets confirm what you had suspected is true: neither New York nor Chicago is big enough for both you and your competition. Chicagoans clearly prefer the rich heartiness of your deep-dish pizza, whereas New Yorkers go for the light, flaky crust of your chief rival. In time, you feel, the battle of New York could be won, but you are pretty sure the competition feels the same way about Chicago. You can save transportation and assorted costs by pulling out of New York and concentrating on the Windy City, but you don't want to give up a marginally profitable operation in the Big Apple unless you get some concessions. Should you

▶ **A**

Expand your Chicago operations and gradually withdraw from New York?

or

▶ **B**

Begin by withdrawing gradually from New York and use the added capital to finance expansion in Chicago?

or

▶ **C**

Announce that you are consolidating your hold on Chicago but reducing the extent of your commitment in New York?

⟶

Solutions #31: **A Pizza the Action**

A Expand your Chicago operations and gradually withdraw from New York?

▶ **-1 point** Although you know what your plans are, your chief competitor doesn't, and it is certain that he or she will view your expansion in Chicago as a hostile move. There is no reason to suspect that your competitor can divine your market intentions, and he or she may escalate hostilities by initiating a price war in Chicago, where you have more to lose. This may benefit the pizza-loving residents of the Windy City, but it certainly won't do you any good.

B Begin by withdrawing gradually from New York, and use the added capital to finance expansion in Chicago?

▶ **1 point** This line of action sends a different signal and is certainly far less likely to precipitate hostilities. However, by starting your campaign with a retreat you are signaling weakness, and your rival may decide that it's time to go for the kill. By the time the two of you get your signals straight, substantial damage to both parties may have taken place.

C Announce that you are consolidating your hold on Chicago but reducing the extent of your commitment in New York?

▶ **5 points** This plan gives you the best chance of achieving your goals. You have sent a clear signal that you are interested in a move that not only increases your own profitability, but may increase your competitor's as well, enabling both of you to find a win-win solution, a solution in which you both win. He or she will see that an offer has been made that can't be refused.

Score _____   **Running Score for Part I** _____

━━━━━━━━━━━━━━━━━━━━━━━━━━━▶ **THE BOTTOM LINE**

Sending clear market signals may prevent costly misunderstandings. There are times when silence is far from golden.

Scenario #32

Bright Lights

Ever since it was discovered that fluorescent lights are more energy efficient than incandescent ones, the profit picture in the fluorescent light industry has brightened considerably. The industry is dominated by four or five major players, and your firm is currently number three but intends to try harder. However, numbers one and two are heavy hitters with whom you don't want to tangle; cross them, and they could make it very difficult for you. What you have to do is scout around to improve your situation without doing anything to create major problems for the industry leaders. Should you

▶ **A**

Look for ways to cut your costs so that you can price your own lights more competitively and grab a greater market share?

or

▶ **B**

Launch an aggressive advertising campaign to try to get your name up in lights, preferably fluorescent ones?

or

▶ **C**

Fund a study to locate areas currently using incandescent lamps, which would benefit by a switch to fluorescent ones?

⟶

Solutions #32: **Bright Lights**

A Look for ways to cut your costs so that you can price your own lights more competitively and grab a greater market share?

▶ **1 point**   While it's never a bad idea to try to cut your own costs, under no conditions should you use the savings to cut prices, as this could easily lead to industry instability. It's best to simply let the savings from cutting costs hit the bottom line directly. Price wars leave everyone in the same relative position, but at a lower profit margin.

B Launch an aggressive advertising campaign to try to get your name up in lights, preferably fluorescent ones?

▶ **2 points**   You have to tread a fine line here, as you want to improve your own situation without angering the industry giants. If this flank attack succeeds, the industry leaders may view this as a result of the campaign run by your advertising agency. They might be more likely to take their hostility out on their own advertising agencies rather than on you.

C Fund a study to locate areas currently using incandescent lamps, which would benefit by a switch to fluorescent ones?

▶ **5 points**   This nonthreatening move is clearly the pick of the litter. In your position, it is far healthier to create new areas of demand than to try to take market share away from those who are stronger. There is also the possibility that you may be able to differentiate your product, or that you may locate a niche that is too small for them to enter profitably.

Score _____   **Running Score for Part I** _____

━━━━━━━━━━━━━━━━━━━━━━▶ **THE BOTTOM LINE**

When you are not a major power in an industry, it is possible you may find a niche just your size, into which the larger competitors cannot comfortably fit. A burrow that is too small for a fox might be ideal for a rabbit.

Scenario #33

High Flyers

It would seem that you should be flying high as one of the leaders of the airline industry, but the truth is that you've had your problems. The performance of your company has been nothing to brag about, and the industry as a whole is undergoing difficult times. There are enough total passengers flying, and enough cargo being shipped, for you to make a profit if you can get more than your current share of each. This is not so easy, because it's getting harder and harder to tell one airline from another. Does your best chance lie in

▶ **A**

Cutting passenger fares along some of your less-successful passenger routes in order to fill up your planes?

or

▶ **B**

Looking for points of comparison where your airline stands out and running an advertising campaign based on that?

or

▶ **C**

Expanding service to other airports, maybe even to other countries, though you're fairly well extended already?

⟶

Solutions #33: **High Flyers**

A Cutting passenger fares along some of your less-successful passenger routes in order to fill up your planes?

▶ **–I point**   At first sight, it looks like a great idea, until you consider the consequences. The problem is that the airline industry is an oligopoly and consists of interlocking entities, not isolated ones. If you cut fares on your unprofitable routes, other airlines will cut fares on theirs, and their unprofitable routes just happen to be your profitable ones. This starts a price war, and everybody gets hurt.

B Looking for points of comparison where your airline stands out and running an advertising campaign based on that?

▶ **5 points**   The best of a poor assortment of choices. You have to find some way to make customers demand your airline, not simply the first flight available. The classic dimensions of product differentiation for airlines are such aspects as service, safety, and on-time percentages. If it weren't for phrases such as "the friendly skies," how would anyone ever know which airline was which?

C Expanding service to other airports, maybe even to other countries, though you're fairly well extended already?

▶ **0 points**   Expansion can be a good idea for a growing air-line, but for one that is fighting to stay in the black, it is rather like an army advancing beyond the point where it can be comfortably supplied.

Score _____   **Running Score for Part I** _____

━━━━━━━━━━━━━━━━━━━━━━━━▶ **THE BOTTOM LINE**

If you can neither achieve low-cost leadership nor attract a particular sector of the market, your only recourse is to create a way to differentiate your product from its competitors. Sometimes the only way to tell one twin from another is by what each is wearing.

Scenario #34

Plumber's Helper

There's nothing especially glamorous about plumbing fixtures, but everybody needs them. As a result of thirty years of hard work, you have built a local plumbing fixtures business into the only nationally recognized retail chain. Expansion prospects are quite good, and you have visions of an empire stretching from sea to shining sea. Or you did until last year, when some TV actor who plays a plumber on a sitcom managed to get funding from somewhere or other and opened stores in New York, Chicago, and Los Angeles, threatening some of your most profitable outlets. Something has to be done and soon, otherwise your plans of empire could go down the drain. Should you

▶ **A**

Immediately cut your prices to the bone in New York, Chicago, and Los Angeles, letting them know that you're playing for keeps?

or

▶ **B**

Attempt to make up your recent loss in profits by expanding to cities where you will be only locally contested?

or

▶ **C**

Go for a national advertising campaign to counter the name recognition that is this actor's only advantage?

→

Solutions #34: **Plumber's Helper**

A Immediately cut your prices to the bone in New York, Chicago, and Los Angeles, letting them know that you're playing for keeps?

▶ **5 points**   In case you don't realize it, unconditional war has already been declared, and you're looking at the plumbing equivalent of Pearl Harbor. If you don't retaliate and fast, you could find yourself in a lot of trouble. You have to let the enemy know you intend to utilize the brute force approach and fight them every inch of the way, and an unconditional price war is the biggest gun in your arsenal. The market signals you send, in addition to being very costly to your competitors, will be a strong deterrent against future challenges. You also have the advantage of running a price war in three cities, which represent your competitor's entire market, while you can fund the losses there from your other stores.

B Attempt to make up your recent loss in profits by expanding to cities where you will be only locally contested?

▶ **1 point**   The major problem with this move is that if you act as if nothing is happening, you are inviting everybody who can tell a socket wrench from a light socket into the plumbing fixtures business. While this move is not running up a white flag of surrender, you are certainly turning the other cheek, when this is the time to do unto others before they do unto you.

C Go for a national advertising campaign to counter the name recognition that is this actor's only advantage?

▶ **-2 points**   This will make two people very happy; the account executive in the advertising agency with whom you contract and the actor himself. When you are the strongest competitor in a battle for market share, use your strength quickly and fully.

Score _____   **Running Score for Part I** _____

━━━━━━━━━━━━━━━━━━━━━━━━━━━━▶ **THE BOTTOM LINE**

Whenever you find yourself in a life-or-death struggle, haul out the heaviest artillery in your arsenal. As Vince Lombardi said, winning isn't the most important thing, it's the only thing.

Scenario #35

Advance Info

All's fair in love and war, and part of the way into producing your new winter line, you have managed to obtain photos of your chief rival's top secret, high-fashion coats for the upcoming winter. Despite the fact that you started production sooner and can produce coats for lower prices, your rival's design is superior, and you suspect the majority of the buyers would probably opt for your rival's coat. Proper use of the information you have obtained can nullify some of your rival's design advantage, and so it is up to you to figure out how to use it so as best to freeze your rival out of the winter coat market. Should you

▶ **A**

Offer the buyers special deals and get them to load up their inventory with your coats?

or

▶ **B**

Start from scratch and try to find a new design incorporating some of the best elements of your rival's coat?

or

▶ **C**

Go for a deliberate rip-off of your rival's coat, which you can produce at a lower price?

→

Solutions #35: **Advance Info**

A Offer the buyers special deals and get them to load up their inventory with your coats?

▶ **5 points**   Your choices are never ideal when you are in a disadvantageous position, but this is the best of a poor lot. Since you can produce coats more economically, you are using your own strength in a constructive fashion. The ideal situation would be to have a superior design at a more economical price, but business consists of playing the cards dealt to you in the wisest manner, not wishing you were dealt a better hand.

B Start from scratch and try to find a new design incorporating some of the best elements of your rival's coat?

▶ **0 points**   This move would throw away two of your biggest advantages. By changing horses in midstream, you are negating your cost advantage, as well as the fact that you could have hit the market first. Also, can you really be sure that you will design a superior coat?

C Go for a deliberate rip-off of your rival's coat, which you can produce at a lower price?

▶ **–2 points**   Not only does this move negate your cost and time advantage, it has other drawbacks as well. When you come out with an obvious copy, your rival will know that there is a leak somewhere and will make every effort to plug it, so you may never again get advance information. There is also a chance that you may find yourself on the wrong end of a lawsuit.

Score _____   **Running Score for Part I** _____

━━━━━━━━━━━━━━━━━━━━━━━━━━━━━━▶ **THE BOTTOM LINE**

When you are faced with a losing situation, be willing to accept small losses rather than attempt radical action to create a winning one. Trying to prevent the toast from falling buttered side down onto the table can sometimes make it fall buttered side down onto the carpet.

Scenario #36

Dental Exam

It may not win you the Nobel Peace Prize, but you have just invented something that should be a boon to humanity: a disposable, biodegradable toothbrush. There's not even a whisper of anything like it on the market, and it can be sold at a competitive price. In brushing up on the toothbrush market, you have discovered that there are several firms, each with a fairly large share of the market. You have received offers of financing and overtures from toothbrush manufacturers, and you are almost sure to make a bundle, but whether it's a big bundle or a little bundle depends on how you assess the impact of your discovery on other firms. Are you most likely to clean up by

▶ **A**

Obtaining financing, establishing a small company, and entering the market as an independent entity?

　or

▶ **B**

Subcontracting to supply your toothbrushes to one of the major toothbrush manufacturers?

　or

▶ **C**

Selling the rights to your discovery on the open market, taking the money, and moving on to something else?

⟶

Solutions #36: **Dental Exam**

A Obtaining financing, establishing a small company, and entering the market as an independent entity?

▶ **5 points**   In a close horse race, this is the winner by a nose. The major players are unlikely to react by entering the market immediately because every disposable toothbrush that they sell diminishes the number of their standard toothbrushes that they would sell. Your chief competitors may wish to retaliate, but they will be faced by an inability to pinpoint the most effective way to do this, and it will also be some time before they figure out what to do. Before you make this move, though, make sure that you can find distribution and shelf space!

B Subcontracting to supply your toothbrushes to one of the major toothbrush manufacturers?

▶ **4 points**   Although you will limit the potential profit you will make this way, it's less risky than trying to bring a new product to market on your own. A major company can do a better job of promoting this product than you could, but their incentive to do so may be lacking because they might perceive it as a threat to their established market.

C Selling the rights to your discovery on the open market, taking the money, and moving on to something else?

▶ **2 points**   Risk-free money always has a certain appeal to it, and not only would you avoid the risk, you would avoid a lot of the potential hassles that always attend start-up operations. If you are not the entrepreneurial type, this might be the right move, but you'll have to say "Sayonara" to the big score.

Score _____   **Running Score for Part I** _____

━━━━━━━━━━━━━━━━━━━━━━━━━━━━▶ **THE BOTTOM LINE**

Production of a substitute may encounter minimal competition because other manufacturers may perceive that by producing and marketing the substitute, they would be competing with themselves. There's not much incentive to rob Peter to pay Paul, if Peter and Paul have a joint checking account.

▶ ▶ ▶ ▶ ▶ ▶ ▶ ▶ ▶ ▶ ▶ ▶ # So How Are You Doing?

If you have been keeping a running score, you might cast a glance at the table below to get an idea how you are doing.

Instead of interviewing you for a job, the CEO of a large chain of department stores has asked you to go through the scenarios in Part I of this book.

If Your Score for Part I Is	The CEO Wants You to
▶ Over 125	Manage the West Coast region
▶ Between 90 and 124	Manage the California stores
▶ Between 55 and 89	Manage the Los Angeles store
▶ Between 20 and 54	Manage the toy department of the Los Angeles store
▶ Less than 20	Be a good customer

PART II

The Players and Their Relationships

4

Relations with Customers and Suppliers

THE ISSUES

All firms purchase and sell goods or services and thereby exercise power over and are vulnerable to the power of customers and suppliers. This relative power can be a dominant variable in the long-term success of a company. Therefore, analysis of the factors relevant to negotiating power is necessary before a firm chooses its customers and important suppliers.

Analysis of Customers

Ideally, a firm would like to sell its products or services to loyal customers who will remain happily oblivious to both potential substitutes and price changes, and it would like to purchase its supplies from companies who will value its purchases so strongly that they will be fearful of doing anything to disturb the current relationship. Just as the advice to buy low, sell high is easy to state but difficult to implement, it is often difficult for a company to arrange to sell to ideal customers and purchase from ideal suppliers.

A firm can significantly reduce its vulnerability to the power of customers through judicious selection of those customers. While customers will rarely be ideal, some possess characteristics that make them significantly more attractive. A company whose purchasing needs specifically match the unique capabilities of a supplier's product or service

91

is one obvious example. Sellers would also prefer customers who are not sensitive to price changes in the seller's product or service.

Different factors contribute to price sensitivity. Firms are obviously quite sensitive to changes in the price of the goods or services making up a substantial percentage of their costs. Some firms are not as price sensitive as others because they can easily pass on increased costs to their customers.

Other customer characteristics may also be highly desirable to suppliers. A buyer who would have to incur high switching costs, perhaps by being forced to redesign its own product if it decided to purchase from one of the seller's competitors, is obviously highly attractive to a seller. The buyer–seller relationship involves negotiation, and successful negotiation often involves intelligence (in the military sense). A potential buyer who does not have easy access to other sellers and who is relatively uninformed about his seller's costs and margins will negotiate with less acumen.

The firm's own strategic position may significantly determine its power vis-à-vis customers. Consider two different firms, one of which is pursuing a low-cost producer strategy and the other a narrow market-focus strategy. A large, price-sensitive customer would be unattractive to the latter firm but might be highly attractive to the former. Another possibility is that the threat of forward integration, which occurs when a company owns a firm that buys its products, can greatly reduce the upstream firm's dependence on its current customers.

Analysis of Suppliers

What is ideal for a supplier is obviously disadvantageous for a customer, and vice versa. As a result, the analysis of suppliers simply reverses the roles discussed in the analysis of customers.

The strategic position occupied by the potential supplier firm can be of paramount importance in determining characteristics of favorable suppliers. For instance, a large, price-sensitive firm can find obvious advantages in buying from low-cost producers, but there are drawbacks as well. If the supplier firm should threaten a price increase (and unless other low-cost suppliers can step in to fill the void) the purchasing firm must resign itself to paying more. On the other hand, purchasing from a supplier who focuses on your niche may place him or her at your mercy, especially if there are few buyers and many suppliers in that niche.

In the same category as the threat to customers of forward integration is the threat to suppliers of backward integration. Backward integration occurs when a firm acquires a supplier firm. By so doing, a company can increase its power with respect to its current suppliers.

Changes in Relative Power

The relative power of customers and suppliers can change significantly over time. For example, technology changes can make a supplier's product less useful, thereby reducing its negotiating power. Such changes can also significantly change entry barriers into the industry, consequently increasing or decreasing competition and changing the balance of negotiating power. Changing tastes and prices will affect the patterns of demand over time and strongly affect the relative power of customers and suppliers. Switching costs typically decrease over time, giving buyers a relative advantage over sellers.

The passage of time can also significantly alter the relationship between buyer and seller due to differing growth rates of the two firms. A buyer whose business is expanding rapidly will obviously need increasing quantities of the goods or services being supplied. Unless the seller's capabilities grow to match the buyer's needs, the buyer will be forced to look elsewhere. Additionally, the relative negotiating power of the buyer will have increased in the interim. Sellers must pay close attention to those factors that control the growth of the buyer, to the growth rate of the industry segment in which the buyer belongs, and to the relative market share likely to be controlled by the buyer in the foreseeable future.

Although customers and suppliers have antithetical interests, they also have powerful common interests. The customer's competitive success in some measure determines the supplier's success. Therefore, the sharing of technology and cooperation to reduce costs is often in the interest of both firms.

Scenario #37

Over Easy

They say that one can't make an omelet without breaking eggs. You certainly hope that's the case and that people make a lot of omelets because your tough-minded approach to keeping costs down has made you the most efficient egg producer in the West. Your other competitors are scrambling to catch up with you, as they attempt to incorporate some of your cost-cutting ideas. You want to maintain your profits and your leadership, and one way of doing this is to make sure that you sell to those chains of supermarkets that have the most favorable buyer characteristics. Should you sell to

▶ **A**

A relatively large number of small chains, so that each chain represents a small portion of your sales and thus has little negotiating advantage?

or

▶ **B**

Several large chains, simplifying the delivery and scheduling problems?

or

▶ **C**

The largest supermarket chain you can find, which will buy all your eggs, optimizing delivery and scheduling problems but conceivably handing the chain a negotiating advantage?

→

Solutions #37: **Over Easy**

A A relatively large number of small chains, so that each chain represents a small portion of your sales and thus has little negotiating advantage?

▶ **–1 point**   The key point to be grasped is that when you occupy a position of low-cost leadership, you are always dealing from strength. This is not a situation in which you have to worry about minimizing the negotiating advantage of your potential buyers.

B Several large chains, simplifying delivery and scheduling problems?

▶ **2 points**   The more that you can cut down your costs that are peripheral to the egg business itself, the greater will be your profits. Since you are the low-cost leader in egg production, you should now be concentrating on reducing your costs in other areas of the business, in order to increase your profits. Besides, it might be possible to use these reduced costs to gain an even larger market share.

C The largest supermarket chain you can find, which will buy all your eggs, optimizing delivery and scheduling problems but conceivably handing the chain a negotiating advantage?

▶ **5 points**   Now is the time to put all your eggs in one basket. It is greatly to the advantage of a large buyer to buy from the low-cost leader, so you are actually the one with the negotiating advantage in this position. The risk of selling to one large buyer is substantially reduced when you are the low-cost leader.

Score _____

➤ **THE BOTTOM LINE**

The negotiating advantage of a large buyer is greatly reduced if he or she is dealing with the low-cost leader. You can save a lot of money if you save a few pennies on a large number of transactions.

Scenario #38

Due Processors

Custom Chips, a medium-sized electronics firm specializing in customized microprocessors for industrial applications, has had several good years in a row, and long-range forecasts see continuing increased demand for its product. As head of sales you are reviewing three potential exclusive contracts with three different firms, all of which have approximately the same profit margin. You are growing and have to consider whether it is better to tie up with a company whose growth will match yours or whether it would be better to have surplus capacity with flexibility for future deals. With this in mind, should you sell to

▶ **A**

A major automobile manufacturer, which wants you to supply chips that will simultaneously minimize exhaust pollutants and increase fuel economy?

or

▶ **B**

A midlevel electronic entertainment firm, which will use your chips to handle the control of programmable combination AM–FM radio, cassette deck, turntable, and CD units?

or

▶ **C**

An up-and-coming supplier of industrial lasers, which currently is heavily involved with electro-optical bar code readers for supermarkets?

⟶

Solutions #38: **Due Processors**

A A major automobile manufacturer, which wants you to supply chips that will simultaneously minimize exhaust pollutants and increase fuel economy?

▶ **5 points** The auto industry is mature, competition is fierce, and growth is limited. Why, then, should you happily embrace this alternative? Despite these drawbacks, this industry is so big that the potential growth for YOUR product is virtually unlimited.

B A midlevel electronic entertainment firm, which will use your chips to handle the control of programmable combination AM–FM radio, cassette deck, turntable, and CD units?

▶ **I point** Electronic entertainment is certainly on the increase and shows no signs of letting up. Additionally, there is always the possibility that the firm may go into other areas of electronics (such as TV), and your orders may increase.

C An up-and-coming supplier of industrial lasers, which currently is heavily involved with electro-optical bar code readers for supermarkets?

▶ **3 points** As an industry, lasers have shown substantial growth, and there are applications for inexpensive, medium-priced, and expensive lasers. Not only is the industry doing well, but the company to which you will be selling is itself dynamic; so this offers a good chance for an increase in the future demand for your product.

Score _____   **Running Score for Part II** _____

━━━━━━━━━━━━━━━━━━━━━━━━━━━━━━▶ **THE BOTTOM LINE**

If your business is planning to grow, it is much safer to do so when you have an assurance of future buyers for your product. It is much better to meet firm demand with flexible supply than flexible demand with firm supply.

Scenario #39

Generation Gap

Hardrives Incorporated, a firm for which you are the sales manager, has just developed what promises to be the Lamborghini of hard drives for midsized computers and mainframes. Your hard drive will set the standard in the industry for generations to come. Unfortunately, a computer generation usually lasts only three years or so, and it's up to you to create a loyal base of quality buyers so that you don't get bagged by an upcoming generation gap and left with a lot of Lamborghinis on your hands. Does your best bet lie in ·

▶ **A**

Finding a major manufacturer of computers, which will contract for the majority of your output and will design its computers to take advantage of your unique features?

or

▶ **B**

Finding a major manufacturer of computers, which can be persuaded to purchase all your initial output at a volume discount so you will maximize your profits at the start?

or

▶ **C**

Finding a horde of small buyers, each of whom can now generate machines designed for particular uses?

$\longrightarrow$

Solutions #39: **Generation Gap**

A Finding a major manufacturer of computers, which will contract for the majority of your output and will design his computers to take advantage of your unique features?

▶ **5 points** This is a dream come true. Ideally, you would like to be assured of a buyer that will not only guarantee to purchase all of your output, but will design its computer in such a fashion that it is locked into using your hard drive. This will reduce the intrinsic bargaining power of this buyer and is as close as you can come to being in seller's nirvana.

B Finding a major manufacturer of computers, which can be persuaded to purchase all your initial output at a volume discount, so you will maximize your profits at the start?

▶ **3 points** This is certainly not a bad position to be in, as you are now guaranteed to hit the ground running. At least for today, you have found a good match of purchasing needs relative to your firm's capabilities. Admittedly, there is no guarantee what tomorrow will bring, but while you are enjoying current profits you can scout around for future buyers.

C Finding a horde of small buyers, each of whom can now generate machines designed for particular uses?

▶ **2 points** On the plus side, no one buyer will wield an undue amount of power in negotiating with you. On the minus side, it's virtually certain that not all of today's buyers will be buyers tomorrow. However, some lost revenue will be retrieved because some of today's buyers will doubtless have gotten larger. That's good, but there goes your negotiating advantage.

Score _____   **Running Score for Part II** _____

━━━━━━━━━━━━━━━━━━━━━━▶ **THE BOTTOM LINE**

An ideal buyer not only will purchase all your output but will make his or her own success dependent on the goods or services you supply. Nothing is as heartwarming as true love.

Scenario #40

Couch Potatoes

There are those who say that America is turning into a nation of couch potatoes. You certainly hope that this is true because you play a leading role in the creation of couch potatoes by manufacturing remote control devices. You're good at what you do, and your product is much in demand. The truth is that it's almost too much in demand, as you could sell more remote control devices than you can produce. Everybody's happy now, but will they be the next time you negotiate a contract? The threat of a labor strike and an increase in the price of electronic components threatens to force you to raise your prices. These worries are uppermost in your mind, as you try to decide whether to sell to

▶ **A**

A manufacturer of remote control toy automobiles, which wants relatively simple remote control devices.

or

▶ **B**

A leading manufacturer of videocassette recorders, which wants a more complicated one.

or

▶ **C**

An up-and-coming manufacturer of digitized big-screen televisions, which wants a remote control device similar to the one needed by the manufacturer of videocassette recorders.

⟶

Solutions #40: **Couch Potatoes**

A A manufacturer of remote control toy automobiles, which wants relatively simple remote control devices.

▶ **I point**   One of the advantages of dealing with this particular manufacturer is that if things go well, it will obviously want large orders. However, the other side of the coin is that the remote control device is probably a fairly substantial part of the overall cost of the toy, and if you are forced to boost your prices, this manufacturer may look elsewhere.

B A leading manufacturer of videocassette recorders, which wants a more complicated one.

▶ **2 points**   While the remote control device is an important part of a videocassette recorder, it's obviously not the most expensive component. If the manufacturer has a good year, it obviously won't worry too much if the price of a relatively small item has to be raised.

C An up-and-coming manufacturer of digitized big-screen televisions, which wants a remote control device similar to the one needed by the manufacturer of videocassette recorders.

▶ **5 points**   You're dealing here with an almost ideal customer, who is obviously doing well. Equally important, the component that you are supplying is almost a negligible expense in terms of the overall picture. As a result, this customer is more likely to be relatively insensitive to price changes than either of the others. Sign the customer up before he or she looks elsewhere.

Score _____   **Running Score for Part II** _____

━━━━━━━━━━━━━━━━━━━━━━━━━━▶ **THE BOTTOM LINE**

The price sensitivity of a buyer to the price of an item is directly proportional to that item's percentage of the total expense. An automobile manufacturer is going to be much more concerned with the cost of the engine than with the cost of the steering wheel.

Scenario #41

Mice Work

As the chief purchaser for one of the nation's largest medical research facilities, you can't be accused of running a Mickey Mouse
operation. However, the head of operations has been doing a lot of
complaining recently about unnecessary expenses. It seems that
much of the laboratory's work requires the use of genetically identi-
cal mice, but different divisions of the laboratory are buying different mice from different suppliers. The need for mice from the same
clone to continue your research is nibbling away at your profits. It's
up to you to find a way to take effective countermeasures. Should
you

▶ **A**

Cut down the number of different suppliers and increase the
number of mice purchased from each to get a quantity discount?

or

▶ **B**

Establish standard genetic specifications to which potential sellers
must adhere, thus preventing any particular firm from putting
the squeeze on you?

or

▶ **C**

Attempt to develop an in-house project so that you can supply
your own mice?

⟶

Solutions #41: **Mice Work**

A Cut down the number of different suppliers and increase the number of mice purchased from each to get a quantity discount?

▶ **1 point**   On the surface, it looks good. Fewer suppliers should mean fewer contracts and fewer hassles, and nobody ever thumbed their nose at a quantity discount. Beneath the tranquil surface, though, trouble could be brewing. A large supplier has potential leverage, so you want to be careful about this. Especially dangerous is the fact that experiments requiring mice from the same clone will lead to difficulties as far as switching suppliers is concerned.

B Establish standard genetic specifications to which potential sellers must adhere, thus preventing any particular firm from putting the squeeze on you?

▶ **5 points**   This is a standard maneuver to prevent any particular supplier from gaining negotiating leverage. Because each supplier would have to meet the same criteria, no one supplier would be able to insinuate himself or herself into a position of indispensability. By standardizing criteria, you have eliminated product differentiation and reduced potential switching costs.

C Attempt to develop an in-house project so that you can supply your own mice?

▶ **3 points**   This is certainly an attractive option, as one of the major threats to a supplier is the fear that the buyer may backward integrate him or her out of a contract. However, some threats to integrate backward are more credible than others, and the higher the technology required, the lower the credibility.

Score _____   **Running Score for Part II** _____

━━━━━━━━━━━━━━━━━━━━━━━━━━━▶ **THE BOTTOM LINE**

One way to make sure that no one supplier can gain an undue amount of leverage is to compel all suppliers to adhere to standard specifications. It is both easier and cheaper for a movie producer to find a replacement for one of the extras than for one of the stars.

Scenario #42

Chocoholics

How sweet it is! That's what millions of satisfied customers say when they get a taste of your chocolate. There have been rumors, doubtless spread by disgruntled competitors, to the effect that your chocolate actually contains a narcotic substance because it's so addictive. Your problem is not in making chocolate; by all accounts your chocolate is among the best in the world. What you want to do is find those buyers who will appreciate that fine chocolate is like a vintage wine; there are years when it is necessary to raise the price because of a dearth of fine cocoa beans. Would you prefer to sell your chocolate to

▶ **A**

One of the world's largest candy makers, which will use your chocolate as part of the world's most widely consumed candies?

or

▶ **B**

A maker of premium ice cream, which will use your chocolate to create a chocolate ice cream that costs as much as the equivalent weight of filet mignon?

or

▶ **C**

A leading manufacturer of cocoa, which will mix the chocolate with powdered sugar to make one of the world's most popular cold weather drinks?

⟶

Solutions #42: **Chocoholics**

A One of the world's largest candy makers, which will use your chocolate as part of the world's most widely consumed candies?

▶ **2 points**   Industry leaders are large buyers, but large buyers are well aware of the Golden Rule: the individual with the gold makes the rules. There is also a danger that the candy maker may decide to integrate backward to a greater or lesser extent, which reduces your bargaining power.

B A maker of premium ice cream, which will use your chocolate to create a chocolate ice cream that costs as much as the equivalent weight of filet mignon?

▶ **5 points**   It's always a joy to deal with a buyer who is not only sweet on your product but is also relatively insensitive to price changes. One of the selling points of premium chocolate ice cream is premium chocolate; if the ice-cream manufacturer switches to a lesser grade of chocolate, its rivals will not hesitate to point this out. When a buyer competes with a high-quality strategy, he or she dares not tamper with the quality.

C A beverage manufacturer, which will mix the chocolate with powdered sugar to make one of the world's most popular cold weather drinks?

▶ **I point**   Who ever heard of premium hot chocolate? There is a strong danger here that you are dealing with a customer who is so gauche as to prefer price savings to fine chocolate, which could turn out to be a sticky situation if your price goes up. In your position, the price sensitivity of the potential buyer is an important consideration.

Score _____   **Running Score for Part II** _____

━━━━━━━━━━━━━━━━━━━━━━━━━━━━━━━ ➤ **THE BOTTOM LINE**

A buyer who relies on quality to sell his or her product will pay to maintain that quality. If a headliner is forced to cancel an appearance in Vegas, people who paid $100 for a ticket will demand a refund unless another headliner is found to fill in.

Scenario #43

Future Shock

As the sales manager of a firm manufacturing highly reliable, heavy-duty electric motors, you are suddenly informed by management that because of labor contract renegotiations and anticipated scarcity of certain key components, the prices of these motors are liable to rise during the next few years. It's a good thing you were made aware of this, because you are in the process of selecting the firm to which you will sell the lion's share of the motors you are planning to manufacture. What you would like to find is a customer who is totally insensitive to price changes, but you would settle for one who merely has a thick skin in this regard. Would you prefer to do business with

▶ **A**

A manufacturer of building cranes, which will use the motors to lift I beams for buildings that are under construction?

or

▶ **B**

An automobile manufacturer, which plans to use the motors to position engines in cars as part of their assembly line?

or

▶ **C**

A shipyard freight firm, which intends to use the motors to unload containerized cargo from incoming vessels?

⟶

Solutions #43: **Future Shock**

A A manufacturer of building cranes, which will use the motors to lift I beams for buildings that are under construction?

▶ **2 points**   The advantages here are that the motors will constitute an important part of the machinery, making the crane manufacturer heavily dependent on your product. However, there are always rent-a-crane companies, which can subcontract, and the building industry is subject to periodic downturns.

B An automobile manufacturer, which plans to use the motors to position engines in cars as part of their assembly line?

▶ **5 points**   This is virtually the ideal customer. Because the motors are installed in an assembly line, the entire line will be held up if the manufacturer tries to locate and adapt an alternate motor. Equally important, the manufacturer is not likely to be overly sensitive to price changes in your motor since the cost of using your motor is a relatively small component of the overall cost of the automobile.

C A shipyard freight firm, which intends to use the motors to unload containerized cargo from incoming vessels?

▶ **0 points**   None of the key factors relating to insensitivity of price changes appear to be present. There are always alternative subcontractors, as was the case with the building cranes, and obviously the cost of the relevant hardware is one of the most important components in the profitability of a freight-unloading operation.

Score _____   **Running Score for Part II** _____

━━━━━━━━━━━━━━━━━━━━━━━━━━━▶ **THE BOTTOM LINE**

The greater the degree of dependence of a buyer on your product, the more insensitive he or she will be to price changes. If you are using an electronic heart pacemaker, you're not likely to quibble about a few extra pennies for batteries.

5

Strategic Groups, Barriers, and Industry Evolution

THE ISSUES

Strategic Groups

Companies within an industry can be grouped according to the strategies they pursue. For example, companies in a strategic group may sell a full line of low-cost products, which they assemble from purchased components. Another group may consist of companies selling more differentiated products at a higher price. Still another group may be fully integrated, manufacturing all of its required components. Other groups may emphasize high reliability and high technology or may focus on a specific portion of the market.

The competitors on which a company should focus are those inhabiting the same strategic group. Ford is obviously concerned with the products and policies of Chevrolet, because both are essentially low-cost producers. Neither will spend as much time worrying about what Mercedes is doing, because Mercedes is clearly focusing its attention on a different market sector.

However, analysis must sometimes extend beyond the boundaries of the strategic group. There may be only one fully integrated company (one that manufactures all of its components) in a particular industry, but there may well be other companies trying to capture the same sector of the market. The fully integrated company may have obtained certain advantages through integration, but this should not prevent it from analyzing its competitors.

Barriers

Because of high capital requirements, a slow learning curve, or protected technology, the barriers to entering a group may be high. Such barriers protect the group from firms outside the industry, as well as from firms in another strategic group within the same industry. This situation is obviously to the advantage of firms in the group; it protects the profit and bargaining power of those companies.

On the other hand, the barriers to exiting a group may be high, due possibly to legislative constraints or extensive previous investment of capital or other resources, such as time. Such exit barriers discourage reduction in the number of competitors and obviously work to the detriment of any company occupying that strategic group.

Mobility barriers may exist, which prevent firms already in the industry from changing to a different strategic group. Whereas entry barriers tend to protect all the firms in an industry, intraindustry mobility barriers tend to protect firms occupying a particular strategic group. Such barriers cause some firms to be consistently more profitable than others in the same industry.

Because each strategic group is inhabited by companies pursuing the same basic strategy (e.g. low-cost broad market, differentiated product, etc.), natural barriers exist for a company trying to enter the group. The entering company may need to alter its own administrative structure and manufacturing process in order to change strategies. It may run into problems involving economies of scale or high switching costs. Such costs substantially reduce the probability of successful entry.

Industry Evolution

While individual firms in the industry must be concerned primarily with developments within their particular strategic group, they must also be concerned with broad evolutionary changes in the industry as a whole. As time passes, product and process technology become dispersed, uncertainty is reduced, entry and exit barriers change, and demand may fall. Entry barriers, mobility barriers, and exit barriers typically change markedly as an industry changes from a growth phase to a mature phase, to a declining phase. Technological innovation, as well as passing time, changes in tastes, substitute products, and other factors will contribute to industry evolution. The effect of such longer-term changes must be evaluated and strategies altered to accommodate these changes.

Shared Problems

Strategic groups, barriers, and industry evolution not only affect the relationships among the companies occupying the same strategic group or belonging to the same industry, they also affect the relationships among the individual firms, their customers, and their suppliers. The strategic group occupied by a given firm, for example, may determine to a significant extent the characteristics of its potential customers. Firms pursuing a low-cost strategy will generally be dealing with price-sensitive customers. Firms pursuing a narrow market-focus strategy centering on the production of specialized, high-quality equipment will encounter customers who are relatively insensitive to price, but who will demand specific characteristics, perhaps combined with a greater degree of associated service.

Threats to profitability, such as the threat of substitute products, often affect specific groups in an industry, rather than the industry as a whole, and it is not necessarily evident which strategic group is most likely to come under attack. The pharmaceutical industry, for example, has low-cost producers specializing in widely distributed, inexpensive analgesics such as aspirin. There are now many different aspirin substitutes competing for space on the family medicine shelf. Narrow market-focus groups specializing in the production of rare or costly drugs that are tailored for specific purposes can also be found in the same industry; such firms are always vulnerable to new discoveries in the laboratories of competitors, universities, or research institutions.

This discussion serves to reiterate the continuing emphasis on the three basic questions that each company must continually address. However, problems involving strategic groups, barriers, and industry evolution generally arise only after the company has resolved the fundamental question of its own identity.

While industry evolution may pose difficulties for firms already within an industry, such evolution can open windows of opportunity for firms planning on entering an industry. For such firms an analysis of the barriers and strategic groups within the industry can often influence, in an important way, the basic strategy that the entering firm will eventually decide to adopt.

Scenario #44

Bit Player

In the past few years, you have emerged as one of the premier manufacturers of drill bits. However, you're wondering whether this is the time to expand your product line by manufacturing drills equipped with your drill bits. While top management is extremely enthusiastic about the prospect, you are somewhat more cautious, as you would have to prepare to face some stiff competition. Nonetheless, management wants you to go for it, but there are several different ways to enter this particular market. Should you recommend that the company

▶ **A**

    Attempt to develop a drill that can be marketed nationally under your own name, perhaps preparing the way for a later growth into other types of tools?

      or

▶ **B**

    Develop a quality drill, equip it with your own bits, and manufacture it for distribution under another company's label?

      or

▶ **C**

    Stick with what you do best, namely, manufacture drill bits and await a later opportunity?

⟶

Solutions #44: **Bit Player**

A Attempt to develop a drill that can be marketed nationally under
your own name, perhaps preparing the way for a later growth into
other types of tools?

▶ **–2 points**   A clear case of attempting to run before you
can walk. If you try this, you will have bitten off more than you can
chew, as national chains already have economies of scale, distribution channels, advertising, and other advantages with which you
cannot cope.

B Develop a quality drill, equip it with your own bits, and manufacture
it for distribution under another company's label?

▶ **5 points**   If growth is what you have in mind, this is the
best way to go about it. Let the other company worry about the
problems of marketing and distribution and content yourself with
taking the next step up on the evolutionary ladder. If you succeed
here, consolidate your position and then plan your next advance. At
this stage, you should not worry about problems that might involve
you in undesirable vertical integration but should concentrate on
being an assembler and a good one.

C Stick with what you do best, namely, manufacture drill bits and await
a later opportunity?

▶ **2 points**   While there is nothing wrong with sticking with a
winning strategy, the best time to consider growth is when you are
at the top of your particular heap. If you do not consider growth as
a possibility, you will always be on the defensive, and sooner or later
someone is likely to penetrate your defenses.

Score _____   **Running Score for Part II** _____

━━━━━━━━━━━━━━━━━━━━━━━━━━━━▶ **THE BOTTOM LINE**

All companies seek to grow, but it is important to grow at a rate that
can be accommodated. Take your "Eureka!"s one at a time.

Scenario #45

Disco Fever

Your insistence on hiring only quality technical personnel to work at your small electronics company appears to have paid off, as the head of research has just informed you that his staff has managed to design an inexpensive, high-quality compact disc recorder. Properly handled, this could be a gold mine; to the best of your knowledge, none of the major firms in the industry has achieved this breakthrough. There's no danger of a leak, as the engineers have stock options, and security is tight. Now it's up to you to figure out how to get the most out of this hot new development without getting your fingers burned. Should you

▶ **A**

Conduct discreet negotiations with some of the major manufacturers and have them market it?

     or

▶ **B**

Go into production and spring it on the market before the major firms know what hit them?

     or

▶ **C**

Realize that what you've got is probably too hot to handle and sell it outright to the highest bidder?

⟶

Solutions #45: **Disco Fever**

A Conduct discreet negotiations with some of the major manufacturers and have them market it?

▶ **5 points**   All things considered, this is probably your best bet. The odds are very much against a small company hitting the jackpot twice, and it is up to you to make the most of what is probably your only opportunity to crash the big time. It will probably be exceptionally difficult for a small firm to get the maximum mileage out of a major breakthrough, but you want to make sure that you get a piece of the action. Settle for half of a larger loaf.

B Go into production and spring it on the market before the major firms know what hit them?

▶ **–3 points**   This is certainly the way to make the biggest profit, *if* the major firms don't retaliate. But that's a mighty big *if*. They have top-rated engineers and top-rated lawyers, and that's a pretty formidable lineup. If the United States couldn't protect the secret of the atomic bomb, you might have a hard time defending a compact disc recorder. Big firms can "reverse engineer" your design and produce one nearly overnight.

C Realize that what you've got is probably too hot to handle and sell it outright to the highest bidder?

▶ **2 points**   If this is the worst decision you ever make, you will be a successful manager. You should come out of this rather well, especially if you can generate a bidding war for your product. However, a really hot item can make more than anyone ever dreamed; just look at Trivial Pursuit, for example. Twenty years from now you could still be kicking yourself.

Score _____   **Running Score for Part II** _____

═══════════════════════════════════ ▶ **THE BOTTOM LINE**

Survival in the corporate jungle depends on more than simply developing a good product or service. Contrary to what most people think, just because you build a better mousetrap, the world will not necessarily beat a path to your door.

Scenario #46

Wise Policy

Your huge conglomerate is tempted to enter the automobile insurance business and with good reason: It's hard to pass up selling something that the potential customers are required to buy! Civilization expands with commerce, and the concept of shared risk, which lies at the heart of the insurance industry, has been in large measure responsible for the expansion of commerce. While automobile insurance can be a profitable industry, it is important to look for potential sources of difficulty, and you wish to hire consultants to investigate critical areas. With a limited budget, should you hire

▶ **A**

Actuarial consultants, in order to determine in which region of the country costly accidents and settlements are least likely to occur?

   or

▶ **B**

Legislative experts, to determine in which region of the country legislation is most likely to reduce your profits?

   or

▶ **C**

Additional lawyers, in order to write the contracts that will minimize the amount of claims you will have to pay?

⟶

Solutions #46: **Wise Policy**

A Actuarial consultants, in order to determine in which region of the country costly accidents and settlements are least likely to occur?

▶ **I point**   It is always important to pay attention to costs in any business, but this is not the most critical aspect of the problem. The price of insurance premiums are set sufficiently high to cover the costs, and whether those costs are high or low is simply one of several inputs that determine premiums.

B Legislative experts, to determine in which region of the country legislation is most likely to reduce your profits?

▶ **5 points**   The parameters that define insurance costs, such as likelihood and costs of accidents, vary slowly in comparison with legislation, which may change the nature of the game overnight. In particular, there is the danger that you may be required to do business in an unfavorable climate, and the barriers to exiting may be raised to an uncomfortable height.

C Additional lawyers, in order to write the contracts that will minimize the amount of claims you will have to pay?

▶ **–I point**   With minor variations, the basic legal language of insurance policies is the same for the different competitors in the same market. This is one of the areas that is under intense government scrutiny to prevent the consumer from being defrauded. You may need more lawyers to handle more business but not to make sharper deals.

Score _____   **Running Score for Part II** _____

━━━━━━━━━━━━━━━━━━━━━━━━━━▶ **THE BOTTOM LINE**

Mobility and exit barriers are often subject to the vagaries of governmental intervention. Despite what Bob Dylan once said, sometimes you need more than a weatherman to know which way the wind blows.

Scenario #47

Sharp Move

Because you've made some extremely good decisions when it comes to marketing, an emerging razor blade manufacturer has come to you for advice. They're tired of being cut out of the profits that lie downstream and want to go into manufacturing razors as well as razor blades. However, they are on a somewhat limited budget, and they need some good counsel if this potentially aggressive move is to succeed. They realize that if they enter the wrong section of the market, the results could be disastrous. It is up to you to guide them down the correct path so that, when they go into production, they will have a good chance of success. Should they

▶ **A**

Attempt to develop a cheap razor in order to capitalize on the large segment of the market that regards shaving as a simple necessity?

or

▶ **B**

Try for a specialty razor, such as a high-tech, top-of-the-line product, or possibly a woman's razor?

or

▶ **C**

Attempt to market a self-lathering razor, which their R & D people have just developed and which appears to have no competition?

⟶

Solutions #47: **Sharp Move**

A Attempt to develop a cheap razor in order to capitalize on the large segment of the market that regards shaving as a simple necessity?

▶ **–2 points** Of all the possible courses of action, this is the least attractive. This segment of the market has been filled for more than fifty years by household names such as Gillette, and the economies of scale they have achieved will prevent you from ever becoming competitive in this area. It would be extremely unwise to enter this portion of the market.

B Try for a specialty razor, such as a high-tech, top-of-the-line product, or possibly a woman's razor?

▶ **I point** Slightly better, especially if they can turn out a razor that is to shaving what Rolls Royce is to automobiles. When it would be suicidal to compete with the low-cost leaders, your thoughts must turn to either product differentiation or focusing on a particular market segment. The high margins associated with this sector of the market would make it more likely that a good product would be profitable.

C Attempt to market a self-lathering razor, which their R & D people have just developed and which appears to have no competition?

▶ **5 points** Leading-edge technology is the best chance. If market research demonstrates that there is an interest in the product, the chances improve substantially because there are no competitors. Although market research occasionally sends people barking up the wrong tree (Remember the Edsel?), the easiest niche to occupy is one that has been heretofore vacant.

Score _____   **Running Score for Part II** _____

━━━━━━━━━━━━━━━━━━━━━━━━━▶ **THE BOTTOM LINE**

Almost any risk is preferable than going up against the low-cost leader, who can utilize economies of scale. As a beginning swordsman, it's better to challenge a Mouseketeer than one of the Three Musketeers.

Scenario #48

Smelling Victory

Your company has been one of the leaders in the synthetic fragrance business for years. You have established a comfortable position in the industry, supplying artificial fragrances to companies that use them to enhance perfumes, room fresheners, soaps—everything but Limburger cheese. However, every time you go into a drugstore and see an ounce of some expensive perfume selling for more than the equivalent weight of caviar, your blood pressure goes through the roof. You feel that all they are doing is taking a few pennies worth of chemicals, putting them in a fancy glass bottle, and getting the potential customer to pay highly inflated prices. Should you try to forward integrate by

▶ **A**

Finding some fancy glass bottles, an exotic name, and entering the upper echelons of the perfume market?

or

▶ **B**

Finding some fancy glass bottles, a generic name, and entering the ranks of generic perfumes that "smell just like . . ."?

or

▶ **C**

Taking some of your best rose, floral, and pine scents; buying some aerosol cans; and marketing air fresheners?

$$\Longrightarrow$$

Solutions #48: **Smelling Victory**

A Finding some fancy glass bottles, an exotic name, and entering the upper echelons of the perfume market?

▶ **0 points**   This is so tempting it's scary. The profit margins at this end of the spectrum seem almost astronomical. However, there's more to it than meets the eye (or nose). The top labels are manufactured in Paris or are pitched by a movie star, so there are a lot of added expenses that you don't see. You would have to have Paris connections or find yourself a movie star to even get into the game. This sector of the business is not perfume, it's marketing an image, and you are not yet ready for the requisite vertical integration.

B Finding some fancy glass bottles, a generic name, and entering the ranks of generic perfumes that "smell just like . . ."?

▶ **5 points**   It may not seem as alluring, but this is probably your best bet. Your strength is clearly in manufacturing fragrances, and this segment of the market gives you an opportunity to do what you do best. You could come out smelling like a rose, as it is usually more profitable for a company to utilize its repertoire of strengths to expand rather than to try to expand its repertoire of strengths.

C Taking some of your best rose, floral, and pine scents, buying some aerosol cans, and marketing air fresheners?

▶ **1 point**   The problem with this approach is that you would have to either find someone to manufacture the aerosol cans, competing with firms who are fully integrated and well distributed, or manufacture your own, integrating in a direction to which you are not especially well suited. This doesn't make a whole lot of sense.

Score _____   **Running Score for Part II** _____

━━━━━━━━━━━━━━━━━━━━━━━━━━━▶ **THE BOTTOM LINE**

Your market niche determines whether you are playing a low-cost producer game or a create-an-image marketing game. Make sure you know what the game is before they deal the cards.

Scenario #49

Fine Print

As one of the nation's largest printers you have achieved a measure of financial success by printing those junk mail advertisements that are stuffed into mailboxes from the Atlantic to the Pacific. Profitable, yes. Prestigious, no. You are armed with some of the latest developments in printing technology and would like to take a step beyond the small realm in which you are currently the king. You know there isn't much hope of calling up *Time* or *Sports Illustrated* and successfully grabbing their nationwide printing contract, but there must be a place for an organization as large and efficient as yours. Should you try to get into a larger market by trying to print

▶ **A**

Advertising brochures for various nationwide chains, such as hotels, motels, car rental agencies, and the like?

   or

▶ **B**

Specialty magazines that are nationally distributed but aimed at particular groups, such as sports car enthusiasts?

   or

▶ **C**

Technical books, which often require multiple fonts because they use mathematical and scientific symbols?

⟶

Solutions #49: **Fine Print**

A Advertising brochures for various nationwide chains, such as hotels, motels, car rental agencies, and the like?

▶ **5 points**   This seems the logical line of approach. Because you have already done a lot of junk-mail printing, you already have connections with the advertising community, and it should be easy to put out feelers. Also, what you can do best is utilize economies of scale, and these economies are more effectively wielded by printing a million four-page brochures than an equivalent number of pages in magazines.

B Specialty magazines that are nationally distributed but aimed at particular groups, such as sports car enthusiasts?

▶ **I point**   This is not an unreasonable place to start, especially if you would eventually like to get a shot at printing *Time* or *Sports Illustrated*. However, you cannot utilize your economies of scale as efficiently in a smaller market, and you do not have an immediate entrée into the field.

C Technical books, which often require multiple fonts because they use mathematical and scientific symbols?

▶ **–2 points**   While the profit margins might be higher per book, and printing complex technical books would give you an opportunity to demonstrate your proficiency and technical competence, the fact is that the market for technical books, though national, is small, and would totally negate the economies of scale you can generate. Let specialty shops handle them.

Score _____   **Running Score for Part II** _____

═══════════════════════════════════▶ **THE BOTTOM LINE**

Economies of scale are most productive when combined with strategies aimed at low-cost leadership, rather than product differentiation or focusing on a particular market sector. There is a limit to the number of Rolls Royces that can be sold, but there is no limit on Toyotas.

Scenario #50

Token Resistance

As head of one of the nation's leading suppliers of electrical and electronic equipment, it came as quite a surprise when the high-temperature superconductors were discovered back in 1986. You were quick to realize that such innovations might make current technology obsolete. Fortunately, your company is in an excellent cash position, and there is no resistance on the part of management to creating a research program to investigate this phenomenon. However, leading experts seem to be well grounded in feeling that applications are still ten to twenty years away, and major break-throughs are still needed. It is up to you to construct an intelligent policy dealing with research expenditures. Should you

▶ **A**

Take a small portion of your cash and start a preliminary pro-gram, hoping to gain experience and possibly get lucky early?

or

▶ **B**

Sit back and wait for the uncertainties of the industry to shake themselves out, and then take a full-scale plunge later?

or

▶ **C**

Invest a major amount of research funds now in hopes of leading the race wire to wire?

➡

Solutions #50: **Token Resistance**

A Take a small portion of your cash and start a preliminary program, hoping to gain experience and possibly get lucky early?

▶ **5 points**   This is your best shot at having your cake and eating it too. There are bound to be a lot of mistakes made in the early going, and with a comfortable cash position you can sit back and wait until the technology is mature. On the other hand, you don't want others to get too far ahead of you on the learning curve, so make sure to maintain some involvement in the field. Additionally, there is always the chance that your researchers could be the ones to make a major breakthrough.

B Sit back and wait for the uncertainties of the industry to shake themselves out, and then take a full-scale plunge later?

▶ **2 points**   Your comfortable cash position makes this a reasonable option. The odds are that much of the money spent at the moment will be wasted, at least as far as the final marketable technology is concerned. However, it's sometimes hard to get into a race if you have no horses.

C Invest a major amount of research funds now in hopes of leading the race wire to wire?

▶ **0 points**   While not totally foolhardy, it is usually best to leave the major portion of early risk taking in an immature field to the believers, the monomaniacs with a mission. Let them make the early mistakes, and then pounce.

Score _____   **Running Score for Part II** _____

━━━━━━━━━━━━━━━━━━━━━━━━━▶ **THE BOTTOM LINE**

A well-capitalized leading company generally need not concern itself with the race to develop first-generation technology, but with the race to utilize the later generations. A well-fed tiger need not spend time and energy chasing a scrawny rabbit.

Scenario #51

Soft Landing

When the top managers of the software company, of which you are the research director, were young and when the company was in its infancy, they took risks that would make your hair stand on end. Now that they have gotten older, and the company has become more prosperous, they have become extremely conservative. That's not to say they have become reactionary, as they recognize that in a rapidly changing industry such as theirs, it is necessary continually to be on the alert for new possibilities. Right now they are considering expanding their product line and want your advice. You have to take into account their attitude toward risk, as you advise them whether to enter

▶ **A**

The voice-recognition software game, which everyone agrees will be big in five years, or maybe ten.

or

▶ **B**

The expert-systems software area, which is rapidly expanding into many different areas.

or

▶ **C**

The video games arena, which is currently the largest of the three areas, but every so often shows signs of topping out.

⟶

Solutions #51: **Soft Landing**

A The voice-recognition software game, which everyone agrees will be big in five years, or maybe ten.

▶ **–1 point** For a company willing to take chances, this would be an ideal area, but the risks associated with the developmental stage of an industry are enormous. You could work for years and come up empty.

B The expert-systems software area, which is rapidly expanding into many different areas.

▶ **5 points** The growth period is the least risky time to enter an industry. You can afford an occasional slipup, because the industry's expansion indicates that the demand is outstripping the supply. The reduction of uncertainty that accompanies a product which has gone beyond the developmental stage should make this option attractive to a company with your risk profile.

C The video games arena, which is currently the largest of the three areas, but every so often shows signs of topping out.

▶ **1 point** Although there is a large and established market, and hence a large demand, there is also a large supply (which is perhaps an indicator of coming overcapacity), and you would be entering the shark-infested pool that is characteristic of a mature industry. As a result, the risk parameters during this period are likely to be unacceptable to those who are known to be risk-averse. Industries shake out when demand tops out, and the low-cost producers who have already paid for capital expansion usually walk away with the majority of the marbles. You cannot invest and compete when starting from scratch.

Score _____   **Running Score for Part II** _____

━━━━━━━━━━━━━━━━━━━━▶ **THE BOTTOM LINE**

When an industry is growing, demand is exceeding the supply, so all a company has to do is manufacture products economically. You don't have to be a great gardener to get plants to grow in fertile ground.

Scenario #52

Fatal Distraction

As the head of a successful electronics manufacturing firm, you have been reviewing the track records of products that have recently gone into production. Like Sherlock Holmes spotting the vital clue, you suddenly noticed that there was a common denominator to your few failures: They came in areas in which there were a large number of competitors. Perhaps this occurred because the market survey team persuaded the design team to incorporate the best features of the competition, rather than letting the design team do its thing. Despite this, it was a very good year, and you are looking to expand your product line. However, you want to make sure that you get into an area where you don't run the risk of this type of situation happening again, and the best way would be to avoid areas where there is a lot of competition. With this in mind, should you tool up to manufacture

▶ **A**

Digital audiotape players, a field that is expanding rapidly in Japan but is just getting started here?

or

▶ **B**

Compact disc players, which are growing by leaps and bounds and are showing no signs yet of peaking?

or

▶ **C**

Walkmen personal cassettes and radios, with a huge market but one that has basically stabilized?

$\longrightarrow$

Solutions #52: **Fatal Distraction**

A Digital audiotape players, a field that is expanding rapidly in Japan but is just getting started here?

▶ **5 points**   Given that you do poorly in a competitive environment, you want to do your best to avoid competitors, and the competition is least during the introductory phase of a product. Usually the dominant companies, which have much to conserve, haven't decided to manufacture it yet because they don't know whether it will be a hit or an Edsel.

B Compact disc players, which are growing by leaps and bounds and are showing no signs yet of peaking?

▶ **I point**   From an overall standpoint, the growth phase of an industry is the best time to get in for a variety of reasons, not the least of which is that the industry growth can compensate for errors on the part of the individual company. On the other hand, the competition is fierce during this period, as everybody wants to hop on the bandwagon. Given your company's track record, it would seem that the best strategy for it to pursue would be the early hit-and-run.

C Walkmen personal cassettes and radios, with a huge market but one that has basically stabilized?

▶ **–I point**   When an industry has reached maturity, as the personal cassette and radio industry has, it's shakeout time. The industry rapidly divides into two groups: the movers and shakers, and the moved-out and shook-up. Your history indicates that you are far more likely to be shook than shaking.

Score _____   **Running Score for Part II** _____

━━━━━━━━━━━━━━━━━━━━━━━━━━━━━▶ **THE BOTTOM LINE**

It is just as important to avoid getting into situations that expose your weaknesses as to get into situations in which you can exploit your strengths. Achilles might have done a lot better if he had worn boots.

Scenario #53
Medical Emergency

Nobody could ever say that a profit is without honor. Certainly not the board of directors of the medical equipment manufacturer for whom you are the research director. A couple of recent fiascoes have had a negative impact on the company's profitability, and the board wants you to develop a new product that will have a high probability of contributing quickly to the bottom line. They are willing to throw the considerable resources of the company behind your choice, but make no mistake about it, your head is on the chopping block. The only way to remove it is to manufacture a quick winner. Should you go for

► **A**

Tomographic scanners, a new development that has very high margins but has only just begun to appear on the market?

or

► **B**

Ultrasound diagnostic devices, which are rapidly coming into favor throughout the entire medical community?

or

► **C**

X-ray machines, a mature technology and a large, mature market but one that is not very likely to grow substantially?

⟶

Solutions #53: **Medical Emergency**

A Tomographic scanners, a new development that has very high margins but has only just begun to appear on the market?

▶ **0 points**   You have been given an ultimatum to show a profit, and taking a chance on an industry in its infancy is no way to guarantee that this will happen. Admittedly, if the company were to take a longer view, this could well be the right move, but it's inadvisable considering that you have to produce NOW.

B Ultrasound diagnostic devices, which are rapidly coming into favor throughout the entire medical community?

▶ **5 points**   Nothing in life is guaranteed, but the best shot at immediate profits is to seek a product for which the market is expanding. Expanding markets signify strong demand, so if you can trundle a reasonable piece of hardware out to the showroom, the odds are very good that you'll have all the action you can handle.

C X-ray machines, a mature technology and a large, mature market but one that is not very likely to grow substantially?

▶ **-1 point**   While mature markets are often the ones with the greatest demand for a product, in this phase of industry evolution the supply side of the picture is pretty well covered. The lion's share of the market is going to the established producers, and you are not going to be able to compete with them overnight.

Score _____   **Running Score for Part II** _____

━━━━━━━━━━━━━━━━━━━━━━━━▶ **THE BOTTOM LINE**

The most likely way to make a profit is to supply something for which there is an established and growing market. It's hard to bag your quota where there are more duck hunters than ducks.

Scenario #54

Quality Control

Quality is not your middle name; it's actually your first name. Quality Telephones has been a leader in upper-echelon telephone equipment ever since Uncle Sam broke up Ma Bell. You've done extremely well producing top-of-the-line equipment, and you want to do nothing to jeopardize your good name. It isn't true that the one who steals your purse steals trash, but, let your good name be sullied by putting an inferior-quality piece of equipment on the market, and the opposition would be quick to bad-mouth your entire product line. However, you've had several back-to-back good years, and it's time to put new merchandise into the catalog. Should you try to develop

▶ **A**

Videophones, which are just being introduced but will take the market by storm in five or ten years?

or

▶ **B**

Cellular car phones, the fastest-growing segment of the market?

or

▶ **C**

Multiple-line business systems, which have been in use for some time and are a must for phone-intensive businesses?

$\longrightarrow$

Solutions #54: **Quality Control**

A Videophones, which are just being introduced but will take the market by storm in five or ten years?

▶ **–2 points** These might be just the thing for Buck Rogers or Captain Kirk, but for a company priding itself on delivering top-quality equipment, it's foolhardy to get in at the developmental stage of the industry. During this phase, the technology is undergoing rapid changes, and there are still numerous bugs to be ironed out.

B Cellular car phones, the fastest-growing segment of the market?

▶ **2 points** There has to be a very good reason to avoid getting in during the growth phase of a market, but you have one: quality. The technology still has not reached maturity, and though everybody may want a cellular car phone, they still sound pretty awful, don't work when one drives through a tunnel or under a bridge, and can create a lot of aggravation.

C Multiple-line business systems, which have been in use for some time and are a must for phone-intensive businesses?

▶ **5 points** Bingo! This is the best match of your capabilities with your objectives. You are dealing here with reliable equipment, equipment that is absolutely the lifeblood of whatever company wants the best. You are prepared to give it to them, and they'll be delighted to pay top price for top-of-the-line, reliable technology.

Score _____   **Running Score for Part II** _____

━━━━━━━━━━━━━━━━━━━━━━━━━━━━▶ **THE BOTTOM LINE**

A company focusing on buyers searching for quality is not always well served by entering a growth industry, where quality is sometimes elusive. There is almost no such thing as a young statesman.

Scenario #55

Cost Cutter

Headquarters is sending over Cheapskate Charlie for a few days to take a look at cutting costs in the small kitchen appliances section of your consumer goods manufacturing company. Nobody likes Charlie; the last time he made a visit he recommended reheating yesterday's coffee in order to save money. However, you have to admit that Charlie is good at what he does, which is cutting costs, and headquarters likes to see every section show profits, if at all possible. Charlie may have all the personality of reheated instant coffee, but he's good at making sure that costs are pared to the bone. The question is where to put him. Should you assign him to

▶ **A**

Ultrasonic coffeepots, a newly introduced item that seems to require an overly expensive manufacturing process?

   or

▶ **B**

Microwave ovens, a segment that is growing so fast the cheery bottom line masks occasional slipups?

   or

▶ **C**

Waffle irons, for which the market is relatively stable and which is one of the oldest product lines made by the company?

⟶

Solutions #55: **Cost Cutter**

A Ultrasonic coffeepots, a newly introduced item that seems to require an overly expensive manufacturing process?

▶ **0 points** Not even the most hardheaded company expects that newly introduced products can be produced optimally; that's one of the expected risks that a company takes with such products. In fact, because efficient production typically requires some standardization of specifications, it would be unrealistic to expect optimal efficiency at this stage. Assuming that ultrasonic coffeepots survive birth trauma, there will be plenty of time to standardize and take cost-saving measures when they grab a sizable market share.

B Microwave ovens, a segment that is growing so fast the cheery bottom line masks occasional slipups?

▶ **3 points** It never hurts to cut costs anywhere, and it is possible this may be the most productive area for the few days of Charlie's visit. However, since the industry is still growing and is showing a nice profit, his presence here is clearly not absolutely essential.

C Waffle irons, for which the market is relatively stable and which is one of the oldest product lines made by the company?

▶ **5 points** In this mature industry, there is little product differentiation, and cost cutting may well be the difference between profit and loss. Admittedly, it might also help matters if you could talk headquarters into sending over some experts who might help increase your market share, but since Charlie is what you've got, this is probably the best place to make use of his abilities.

Score _____   **Running Score for Part II** _____

━━━━━━━━━━━━━━━━━━━━━━━━▶ **THE BOTTOM LINE**

Where the demand is growing there is little need to cut costs, but where demand tops out, cost cutting and increased market share become primary goals. The retired person on a fixed income is the one most likely to need to go on a budget.

▶ ▶ ▶ ▶ ▶ ▶ ▶ ▶ ▶ ▶ ▶ ▶ # So How Are You Doing?

Well, nobody said it would be easy. Remember, though, that successful managers are made, not born.

The CEO of the New York business for which you work has decided to establish an incentive plan for managers and potential managers by awarding free trips.

If Your Score for Part II Is	You Will Receive
▶ Over 65	A first-class, round-trip ticket to Paris
▶ Between 50 and 64	A first-class, round-trip ticket to San Francisco
▶ Between 30 and 49	A round-trip ticket to Chicago
▶ Between 10 and 29	A round-trip ticket to Atlantic City
▶ Less than 10	A one-way ticket to Newark

PART III

The Industry and Its Many Phases

6

Coping in a Fragmented Industry

THE ISSUES

A fragmented industry is one composed of a large number of small and medium-sized firms, where no firm holds a dominant position. Such an environment requires different strategies and perspectives than those required in an oligopoly (an industry with a few dominant companies).

Causes of Industry Fragmentation

Fragmentation occurs for many reasons. There may be low entry barriers, which make it easy for a fledgling company to join the industry. There may be high exit barriers, which trap companies already in the industry and make it difficult for them to get out. Additionally, the existence of certain factors, such as potential gain from economies of scale or from the presence of a significant learning curve, may be absent from a fragmented industry. All these conditions work to prevent the emergence of companies that can dominate the industry.

Fragmentation can exist throughout an entire industry or may be concentrated within a particular strategic group. It can exist in either the broad or narrow market-focus sector of the market and is independent of whether the goods or services being produced are low-cost or differentiated.

While it would be unfair to characterize fragmentation as a manifestation of chaotic conditions, the fact remains—many of the most idiosyncratic industries tend to be fragmented. Many industries featuring a high level of creativity, such as art, music, or advertising, are highly fragmented. Industries that attract individuals who value independence are also likely to be fragmented, almost by definition.

Fragmented Industries: A Vital Sector of the Economy

On the other hand, the fact that an industry is fragmented does not imply that the industry is unimportant. Some of the most basic industries, which exist in virtually every country, are fragmented, and are doubtless destined to remain so. Retailing is one notable example; indeed, the American dream of owning a small business exists simply because the retailing industry has relatively low entry barriers. Other noteworthy examples are industries that specialize in a particular service, such as real estate, or distribution-oriented industries such as trucking firms.

Fragmentation not only characterizes certain industries throughout their entire evolution, it is a feature of other industries at particular periods. Often the inception of an industry is marked by fragmentation. During the late 1970s and early 1980s, the personal computer industry was highly fragmented. Although it is still fragmented, the entry of such major companies as IBM, Digital, AT&T, and Zenith makes it considerably less so.

Some industries become substantially more fragmented as they evolve. This can often occur for technological reasons. Indeed, whereas the burgeoning personal computer industry can be regarded as being in its initial phase during the late 1970s and early 1980s, it is possible to regard it as a sector of the computer industry as a whole. In the late 1940s and early 1950s, only the most solidly capitalized companies were able to afford the technology needed to enter the computer industry. The invention of the microprocessor made fragmentation of the computer industry possible, as the level of technology became more and more affordable. Similar developments could be seen in other areas of electronics, such as transistor radios.

The effect of industry fragmentation on a firm's relations with customers and suppliers is pronounced. It is exceptionally difficult to select ideal customers and ideal suppliers when an industry has many competitors. As a result, the negotiating power of a firm in a fragmented industry is likely to be significantly reduced relative to the negotiating power of a firm in an oligopoly.

The Lure of Fragmentation

Many of the characteristics of a fragmented industry may seem unfavorable, but sometimes beauty lies in the eye of the beholder. The absence of significant benefits to be derived from economies of scale or the presence of a learning curve is disadvantageous to the firm that can bring these features into play, but to the individual or firm not possessing such assets, the fragmented industry can offer unparalleled opportunity.

Similarly, the low entry barriers to a fragmented industry are obviously disadvantageous to the firm already entrenched there. To the potential entrant, however, low entry barriers are an obvious invitation.

In general, fragmented industries form a significant portion of the business environment. To the potential entrant not possessing substantial capital or other unusual assets, a fragmented industry can offer the probability of an attractive risk/reward ratio, although possibly not a high probability of success. A firm seeking entry into another industry that either buys from or sells to a fragmented industry enjoys the extra bargaining power that comes in dealing with the many competitors that result from fragmentation.

Taking Fragmentation into Account

The relative importance of the three basic questions that a company must confront depends upon the industry environment. In a fragmented industry, it is clearly less important to pay attention to what a particular competitor or even a group of competitors is doing. While there are obvious exceptions to this rule (a price war among neighboring gas stations is an example), the diminution of the importance of the competitive factor is one of the obvious attractions of a fragmented industry, making it easier for a company to succeed by concentrating on what it is doing.

Coping with fragmentation might involve using multiple decentralized, low-cost operations at different locations, differentiating or specializing a company's product or service, or focusing on a specific portion of the market.

An attractive trap that should be avoided by larger companies in fragmented industries is an attempt to seize a leadership role in the industry by overcoming some of the factors leading to fragmentation. Attempting to implement economies of scale, for instance, in an industry not amenable to such economies can actually be counterproductive, involving large capital outlays for dubious returns.

Scenario #56

Skin Deep

The poet John Keats was a little nineteenth-century when he said that "beauty is truth, truth beauty." A twentieth-century Keats would have said "beauty is profitable, and profits are beautiful," especially if he had taken a look at the bottom line of your nationally franchised chain of beauty salons. However, there is no one so beautiful that he or she cannot be improved by the right hairstyle, and there is no balance sheet so perfect that it cannot be improved by an intelligently conceived and well implemented plan. It is up to you to come up with a policy decision that, when well implemented, will turn your bottom line into a thing of beauty and a joy forever. Should you

▶ **A**

Institute a plan to centralize decisions at the national headquarters?

   or

▶ **B**

Work out an incentive plan for individual establishments, which would reward superior performance?

   or

▶ **C**

Bring in lower-cost personnel and equipment, and improve profits through the time-honored expedient of cutting costs?

⟶

Solutions #56: **Skin Deep**

A Institute a plan to centralize decisions at the national headquarters?

▶ **0 points**   If you make the mistake of trying to impose such detailed controls, you are liable to find yourself in some ugly confrontations with your franchisees. What is beauty in Dallas is not necessarily beauty in Detroit, and close local control is essential to service diverse market needs. The success of your chain depends both on the franchisor and the franchisee. Centralized decision making in a service-oriented business is liable to make the local proprietors very unhappy.

B Work out an incentive plan for individual establishments, which would reward superior performance?

▶ **5 points**   Here is a genuinely beautiful idea, tightly managed decentralization, in which you reward overall results. You are dangling a very attractive carrot in front of your franchisees and their employees. This will enable the national headquarters to be seen as a place from which rewards rather than punishments emanate. It is important to avoid homogenizing the individual units that constitute your business, as this would demonstrate insensitivity to local conditions.

C Bring in lower-cost personnel and equipment, and improve profits through the time-honored expedient of cutting costs?

▶ **-I point**   You do not want to tamper with the nuts and bolts of your success. People go to beauty parlors because they appreciate service and the effect that service has on them, and they are doubtless going to your beauty parlors because they *like* to. If you change a lot of your horses in midstream, your bottom line is likely to show some unattractive losses.

Score _____   **Running Score for Part III** _____

━━━━━━━━━━━━━━━━━━━━━━━━━━➤ **THE BOTTOM LINE**

When looking for ways to improve, never tamper with the elements critical to your success. A hitter who has been hitting the ball on the nose shouldn't change his or her swing.

Scenario #57

Haute Couture

It's been a bad few years for high-fashion designers and not just because the industry seems to have fallen on hard times. Dior, Chanel, and Balenciaga are all looking over their shoulders at YOU. Their sales have fallen while yours have risen fashionably high. While small fashion houses throughout the world have gone belly-up, your star is definitely on the rise, as jet-setters throughout the world are wearing your designs. There is now an opportunity to take over as one of the world's fashion leaders, and while others in your organization are in charge of designing dresses, you are designing something just as significant: policy. Should you

▶ **A**

Take advantage of the collapse in the industry to look for vacated high-fashion niches, such as shoes and accessories?

or

▶ **B**

Buy up the weaker houses and make a strong effort to consolidate a fragmented industry?

or

▶ **C**

Realize that the opportunities for high fashion are decreasing and attempt to expand downward to make a line accessible to the comfortably off as well as the wealthy?

⟶

Solutions #57: **Haute Couture**

A Take advantage of the collapse in the industry to look for vacated high-fashion niches, such as shoes and accessories?

▶ **5 points**   Much though you would like to extend your domain as far as possible, the very nature of your business prevents you from stretching your boundaries too far. In fact, this is the classic mode of expansion for high fashion; it is necessary to maintain a veneer of exclusivity and inaccessibility.

B Buy up the weaker houses and make a strong effort to consolidate a fragmented industry?

▶ **1 point**   This approach might work, but you are always likely to bang up against the following inescapable fact: Expanding production will not necessarily increase profits. In fact, it could even prove counterproductive. Some industries are forever doomed to remain fragmented, and industries marked by heavy creative content belong to this category.

C Realize that the opportunities for high fashion are decreasing and attempt to expand downward to make a line accessible to the comfortably off as well as the wealthy?

▶ **-1 point**   While it is tempting to try to increase your profits by expanding your product line, how do you think Rolls Royce would fare if it put out a subcompact, and everybody had a Rolls Royce in his or her garage? Even if you put out your new line under a different label, the cognoscenti might refuse to buy from a manufacturer so crass as to cater to the *hoi polloi*.

Score _____   **Running Score for Part III** _____

━━━━━━━━━━━━━━━━━━━━━━━━━━━━➤ **THE BOTTOM LINE**

It can be easier to succeed in a fragmented industry by employing a strategy based on product differentiation or focusing on a particular market sector. Just because you can't compete with McDonald's or Wendy's on price doesn't mean that you can't make money selling hamburgers.

Scenario #58

Networking

You can consider yourself both lucky and smart, as you got your degree in EECS (Electrical Engineering and Computer Science, rhymes with "squeaks") at just the right time and have managed to grow your computer and telecommunications company from a local to a regional firm. Things have gone extremely well, and you are now in a position to make a move for national prominence. One way to make such a move is to execute a business coup by creating a nationwide chain of local agencies in a fragmented industry, and introducing the industry to the advantages of consolidation. It's up to you to move into the area most ripe for consolidation. Should you select

▶ **A**

Computerized dating services, figuring that people who need people are the luckiest people in the world?

or

▶ **B**

Computerized casting services, keeping track of who's hot, who's not, and who's available for movies and television shows?

or

▶ **C**

Computerized real estate services, as real estate has been one of the businesses with a continual record of growth?

$\longrightarrow$

Solutions #58: **Networking**

A Computerized dating services, figuring that people who need people are the luckiest people in the world?

▶ **0 points** When planning to consolidate an industry, it is important to ask how the various firms involved in consolidation will benefit. It is difficult to see how computerized dating services, which are essentially local in nature, would benefit, as there are no special services or economies of scale that would be generated.

B Computerized casting services, keeping track of who's hot, who's not, and who's available for movies and television shows?

▶ **I point** This might be a good publicity ploy, since anything involving the entertainment industry receives a lot of media coverage. Actors and members of the entertainment profession are probably more mobile than the average, and an actor might appear in Boston one week and Chicago the next. Nonetheless, the gains effected by your service would probably be marginal.

C Computerized real estate services, as real estate has been one of the businesses with a continual record of growth?

▶ **5 points** It's not the continuous growth that is so appealing but the fact that many real estate purchases are made by individuals who are located in one region but have to move to another. As a result, special services can be designed to appeal to this important group of consumers, and make consolidation appealing to many individual firms.

Score _____   **Running Score for Part III** _____

━━━━━━━━━━━━━━━━━━━━━━━━━━━━▶ **THE BOTTOM LINE**

If there is nothing to be gained from consolidation, there is no incentive to consolidate. People who aren't*in love and can afford to live alone usually do so.

Scenario #59

Paint the Town

You wouldn't think that something could be simultaneously under-appreciated and overvalued, but consider the effect of a fresh coat of paint on a house. You don't notice it so much when it's there, but an unpainted house can stand out like a sore thumb. You own a house-painting company, and you'd like to think that there must be a way to take advantage of your success in the field and perhaps expand or move on to a more secure financial position within the building-contracting industry. You've built up a lifetime of contacts on both the service and supply side of building contracting, and it has occurred to you that there must be a way to capitalize on this. Of course, you'd hate to waste your time, effort, and perhaps even money on a hopeless cause. Should you

▶ **A**

Work out an arrangement with paint supply and hardware stores to obtain their products at reduced prices?

or

▶ **B**

Consolidate within the industry by merging with other house-painting companies in the area?

or

▶ **C**

Form an alliance with companies in other trades, such as carpenters and plumbers, to supply the major part of the work on a house?

→

Solutions #59: **Paint the Town**

A Work out an arrangement with paint supply and hardware stores to obtain their products at reduced prices?

▶ **1 point**   While it's never a bad idea to look for ways to reduce your costs, the reality of the situation is that this course of action will probably be extremely difficult. There are many house-painting companies, and in a fragmented industry buyers have relatively little power, as any one buyer can always be replaced.

B Consolidate within the industry by merging with other house-painting companies in the area?

▶ **1 point**   While there is nothing wrong with this idea, there isn't really a whole lot of incentive for other companies to do this, as there are no economies of scale or similar benefits to be derived. Even though you can focus on a specific geographic area, it will not greatly reduce the marketing or sales activity associated with the individual firms.

C Form an alliance with companies in other trades, such as carpenters and plumbers, to supply the major part of the work on a house?

▶ **5 points**   This is your best bet, although it is certainly not a sure thing. However, contractors will be able to save money by dealing with a central clearinghouse, and this might supply the needed incentive for other companies to join with you.

Score _____   **Running Score for Part III** _____

━━━━━━━━━━━━━━━━━━━━━━━━━━━▶ **THE BOTTOM LINE**

When considering consolidation, ask yourself both "what's in it for me?" and "what's in it for them?" In a good marriage both parties win and create payoffs neither could have without the other.

7

Industry Growth, Maturity, and Decline

THE ISSUES

New technologies, new needs, or changes in taste can create new or rapidly growing industries. In such high-growth industries, strategies are uncertain or changing, and significant opportunities and risks abound.

Emerging Industries, Inception and Growth

The emerging industry offers a fascinating combination of reward and risk. The premium associated with success in this phase of the industry can be astronomical; in this phase it is easy to entertain visions of becoming an Apple or a McDonald's. Inevitably, increased risk goes hand in hand with the possibility of exceptional reward, and in no other phase of the industry is it so hard to identify what strategies will be successful. The price of failure at this stage can be high; if demand fails to materialize for the goods or services, much of the investment may never be recovered.

While early entry may involve high marketing risks because of the uncertainty of product acceptance, it may also offer the clear advantages of low entry barriers and the ability to charge higher prices and create bigger profit margins. Initial costs are high, but they decrease rapidly in the wake of fast learning and improved procedures. Production bottlenecks, high costs, quality problems, and customer confusion may occur because of the pressure to meet the new and growing demand.

In most organisms, a successful birth is followed by a period of rapid growth. Industries in the rapid-growth phase are extremely alluring to potential entrants because of the expansion of demand that characterizes this phase. If the entry barriers are not overly high because of expensive or proprietary technology, there is liable to be a flood of entrants.

Firms in rapid-growth industries, typically with new products, must develop strategies to attract first-time buyers, and induce buyers to switch from existing products. At the same time, these firms attempt to strengthen the industry and their own position. This is a period of time when the firm needs an entrepreneurial chief executive officer, who is a "monomaniac with a mission."

Transition to Maturity

Just as it is impossible for an organism to sustain rapid growth, it is impossible for an industry to maintain increasing demand. Not only will demand eventually level off, but the rapid-growth phase of the industry, which attracted new entrants, plants the seeds of its own destruction as the competition intensifies.

An industry's transition from growth to maturity is a critical period characterized by important strategic and administrative discomfitures for the individual companies. Demand and capacity top out, competition increases, knowledgeable customers seek service and low prices rather than differentiated brands, manufacturing and marketing processes must be made more efficient to reduce costs, the power of buyers increases, and industry profits fall as the fight for market share intensifies. At this stage a company needs a different type of chief executive, a mean, lean, no-nonsense administrator who will implement sophisticated cost analysis and pricing.

Declining Industries

While there are industries such as agriculture, transportation, or communication, which seem fated to remain in the mature phase for the foreseeable future, there are those industries that have ridden the wave, only to see it crest. During this phase of the industry, the primary questions center on survival: Is survival worth the effort, and if it is, how should it be managed?

In a declining industry, one in which sales are permanently decreasing, perhaps because demand for the product is saturated or substitute products are reducing demand, companies must develop decline-phase strategies. Such strategies typically involve reducing product lines and services, as well as expenditures for R & D and advertising, while "harvesting" a maximum portion of the cash flow from the declining business.

However, there are widely diverse circumstances in which industry decline might occur. For example, conditions may vary with respect to the speed of the decline, intensity of competition, height of the exit barriers, or presence of overcapacity. Such differing circumstances might create opportunities for, or require an approach different from, the harvest strategy described in the previous paragraph. In some circumstances it is best to liquidate as soon as possible. In others, building a strong focus on a specific market niche could maintain stable demand. There are even circumstances in which a strong leadership approach, in which a company seizes control of a faltering industry, could be highly profitable. Such an approach might include reducing prices, purchasing competitors, and even investing in R & D for both new products and improved manufacturing processes.

As the nature of the industry changes, the type of chief executive officer required changes as well. The decline phase of an industry requires a chief executive officer who recognizes the current industry predicament and is willing to milk the cash cows rather than the visionary who guided the company during its inception and growth phases.

The State of the Industry: A Dominant Variable

This chapter concentrates on the state of the industry, but there is a high degree of interrelationship between this state, the goals of the individual firm, and the nature of the competition.

The basic strategy that a firm decides to adopt depends in good measure upon the state of the industry. An industry undergoing rapid growth generally allows for all possible strategies; broad and narrow market focus, low-cost production and differentiated product. An industry in the decline phase, however, may find the viability of several of these strategies severely curtailed or eliminated.

The nature of the competition, and the attention it demands, depends on the state of the industry. During the struggle for survival, whether at the outset or when the twilight of the industry's existence arrives, the company must turn inward. At maturity, however, when the demand is no longer increasing, the pressure to improve performance turns outward to market share and the competition.

Scenario #60

Cold Cash

People often ask why a country with the resources of the United States can put an astronaut on the moon but can't cure the common cold. They need ask no longer, for you have come up with a cure for the common cold. True, it doesn't work for everybody, and there are a few annoying but minor side effects that occur occasionally, but when it works, the results are spectacular. The amazing thing is that it can be manufactured from ingredients that are available in bulk quantities and at low prices; you wonder that it took so long to discover it. The question is how best and how soon to exploit your discovery. Should you

▶ **A**

Spend a lot more time in research, attempting to discover a variation that will work for everyone?

or

▶ **B**

Go into production as soon as you clear the regulatory hurdles, including a disclaimer that it doesn't work for everybody and does have a few minor side effects?

or

▶ **C**

Do a little more research to see if you can modify the formula to counteract the side effects?

$\longrightarrow$

Solutions #60: **Cold Cash**

A Spend a lot more time in research, attempting to discover a variation that will work for everyone?

▶ **–2 points** This slow and cautious approach is admirable if you are building a space shuttle or a nuclear reactor, whose failure can have devastating consequences. On a discovery like this, such a delay could be catastrophic. What if somebody discovers that all you have to do is add a tablespoon of something or other to chicken soup?

B Go into production as soon as you clear the regulatory hurdles, including a disclaimer that it doesn't work for everybody and does have a few minor side effects?

▶ **5 points** You have a product that will be so much in demand that you can afford to overlook a few drawbacks. In particular, you want to get *your* name associated with cold cures. Take Xerox and Polaroid to heart; there are some races in which nobody remembers who finished second. When you have achieved a state of the art required to yield significant benefits, get your product on the shelves ASAP.

C Do a little more research to see if you can modify the formula to counteract the side effects?

▶ **–1 point** Picky, picky, picky. Yes, it would be nice not to have to print on the bottle "May cause chronic dandruff," but billions of dollars worth of products are sold each year with skull and crossbones clearly displayed. Faint heart ne'er won fair market.

Score _____   **Running Score for Part III** _____

➡ **THE BOTTOM LINE**

When you have a product that a lot of people will want, get it to market as soon as possible. As Damon Runyon remarked, "The race is not always to the swift, nor the battle to the strong, but that's the way to bet."

Scenario #61

Optical Collusion

When you're a leader in any field, you have to look simultaneously over your shoulder at what your competitors are doing, and keep an eye on future developments. As one of the leading manufacturers of mainframe computers, there is a major development lurking some time in the future: optical computers. Instead of computing with electrons rushing back and forth on microchips, optical computers will use photons of light, and will be over a thousand times faster than the fastest electronic computers. You certainly don't want to find optical computers doing to you what you did to slide rule manufacturers. You have been conducting a small amount of research so as to be competitive on the learning curve, but you still must decide when to enter a very immature technology, which won't come to fruition for at least ten years. Should you

▶ **A**

Invest in a major development program right now, hoping to make the breakthrough that will catapult you to the forefront?

or

▶ **B**

Wait a few years, letting others do the preliminary development work, and then invest in serious R & D when the kettle is starting to boil?

or

▶ **C**

Wait until the technology is sufficiently mature that you can invest in production on a large scale without worrying about obsolescence?

$\longrightarrow$

Solutions #61: **Optical Collusion**

A Invest in a major development program right now, hoping to make the breakthrough that will catapult you to the forefront?

▶ **0 points**   With your leadership status in the field, you are as likely to make the breakthrough as anyone else. However, there is no need to bet on the come, as gamblers say. It is possible that the breakthroughs may be even farther down the line than you expect. In addition, leaders don't have to be innovators; the status quo suits them just fine.

B Wait a few years, letting others do the preliminary development work, and then invest in serious R & D when the kettle is starting to boil?

▶ **2 points**   If you want to take a gamble, this is the most intelligent way to go about it. If the first generation of optical computers turns out to be highly profitable, you will have made a wise decision. However, the odds are somewhat against you, as sophisticated technology usually needs to go through a few generations before the biggest profits are made.

C Wait until the technology is sufficiently mature that you can invest in production on a large scale without worrying about obsolescence?

▶ **5 points**   You certainly don't expect to be anything less than a leader in optical computing, which means you will have to go into production on a large scale. You'd like to make sure that the major bugs have been eliminated, as early entry can be risky in a field where technological change is likely to make early investments obsolete. You are in the fortunate position of being able to afford to sit back and wait.

Score _____   **Running Score for Part III** _____

━━━━━━━━━━━━━━━━━━━━━━━⟶ **THE BOTTOM LINE**

Early entry gives you a better chance of dominating the field, but later entry may give you the assurance that a field exists to dominate. It is almost impossible to be both the first and the best.

Scenario #62

Looking Forward

It took more than three billion years of evolution for animals to develop eyes; but pattern-recognition systems will take only a few more years to hit the market. As a small microelectronics company specializing in vision-related hardware, you don't need 20–20 foresight to be able to see that you are going to have to keep a close watch on this area, as your entire product line could be made obsolete. At some stage, you are probably going to have to invest some major capital, and the big question is whether and when to put your money on the line. Should you

▶ **A**

Take some risks by attempting to get in on the ground floor, realizing that early development of workable systems will not necessarily guarantee that you will become the industry standard?

or

▶ **B**

Hold back, hoard your capital, and wait until the second- or third-generation technology to enter the game?

or

▶ **C**

Sell your current inventory and make plans to go out of business?

➡️

Solutions #62: **Looking Forward**

A Take some risks by attempting to get in on the ground floor, realizing that early development of workable systems will not necessarily guarantee that you will become the industry standard?

▶ **5 points**   A small company in a fast-growing field is in a position where it has to take some intelligent risks, and trying to be one of the first to develop or use leading-edge technology represents intelligent risk taking for a small company.

B Hold back, hoard your capital, and wait until the second- or third-generation technology to enter the game?

▶ **–1 point**   This is probably your worst option. When the time comes for profits to be made from second- or third-generation technology, there are generally only two ways to do so. You either have to be an early leader in the field, and take advantage of this fact, or you have to be a heavy hitter willing to invest big bucks to utilize a mature technology. If you are neither, you stand a good chance of going under.

C Sell your current inventory and make plans to go out of business?

▶ **3 points**   It is not courageous for a penny-ante player to get into a high-stakes poker game, merely foolhardy. This is a tough decision to make, but if you are not willing to take the risks associated with getting in on the ground floor, this is probably your best move.

Score _____   **Running Score for Part III** _____

━━━━━━━━━━━━━━━━━━━━━━━━━━━━▶ **THE BOTTOM LINE**

In a field dominated by big companies, a small company in a market niche poised to undergo a drastic change has to take a disproportionate share of risks to survive. A team that's behind in football has to throw the bomb.

Scenario #63

Setting Sun

As head of one of America's leading automobile manufacturers, you have been seething ever since Japan became a major player in the game. It's possible, however, that the Rising Sun is about to set because recent developments now make it practical to produce an affordable solar-powered car. It's no Maserati, and a subcompact solar-powered car costs twice as much as a conventional car, but it gets an infinite number of miles on a gallon of gasoline because it doesn't use any. The technology is in its infancy, but this is going to revolutionize the car business. Should you

▶ **A**

Make a major commitment now, tool up, and rush into production with the world's first affordable solar-powered car?

or

▶ **B**

Establish a research program to place yourself on the cutting edge of solar technology and go into production somewhat later?

or

▶ **C**

Sit back, wait until the smoke clears and the technology settles down, and then go into production, even though others will have gotten ahead of you?

⟶

Solutions #63: **Setting Sun**

A Make a major commitment now, tool up, and rush into production with the world's first affordable solar-powered car?

▶ **I point** If you can see that there is a market for the car as it now stands, this makes some sense. Additionally, there is always tremendous publicity value in being first. However, if the technology is really changing rapidly, it makes a lot more sense to wait rather than investing in equipment that may soon be obsolete.

B Establish a research program to place yourself on the cutting edge of solar technology and go into production somewhat later?

▶ **5 points** This seems like a very good time to hedge your bets. You don't want to find yourself hopelessly behind when the industry starts booming, so it's a good idea to get involved without taking major risks. Additionally, there is always the chance that your program may make *the* major breakthrough, and you will be in a position to really clean up. There is also the possibility that you may obtain research grant funds to cover the cost, because you are doing something that is beneficial from the standpoint of both energy conservation and the ecology.

C Sit back, wait until the smoke clears and the technology settles down, and then go into production, even though others will have gotten ahead of you?

▶ **2 points** This strategy should show a profit, as you won't be tying up a lot of capital, and with hundreds of millions of potential customers it pays to have a good product rather than be first on the market. Additionally, there is always the chance that an unforeseen development will keep these cars off the road.

Score _____   **Running Score for Part III** _____

➡ **THE BOTTOM LINE**

The larger the firm, the more it is important to be flexible at the start of an operation, because making a large commitment is going to lock you into a course of action. It is far less expensive to pay for information than for mistakes.

Scenario #64

Salt Seller

Salt has an ancient and honored history. A soldier's wages used to be paid in salt, which is where the word *salary* comes from. Nonetheless, too much salt is dangerous, and salt water, which covers most of the earth's surface, is undrinkable unless the salt is removed. This is where you come in. Your firm has finally come up with a cheap desalinization process, which can be used on practically any scale. It's not yet perfect, and there are a few bugs, but you want to move into production so as to establish claim to the process and refine it later. However, you want to make a profit while you are doing this. Should you

▶ **A**

Develop a portable desalinator that can be used by mariners as part of an emergency kit?

or

▶ **B**

Develop a large-scale plant that can be used to desalinize water for irrigation?

or

▶ **C**

Develop medium-sized desalinators to supply fresh water in Third World countries that are in dire need of it?

→

Solutions #64: **Salt Seller**

A Develop a portable desalinator that can be used by mariners as part
of an emergency kit?

▶ **5 points** Certainly the best place to start, as it is usually
easier to implement technological innovations on smaller scales first.
Additionally, the failure of a portable desalinator will not have disastrous financial consequences to either the manufacturer or the
user. It is important to minimize the initial risks so that you'll still
be in the game when it becomes feasible to move to a larger scale.

B Develop a large-scale plant that can be used to desalinize water for
irrigation?

▶ **–1 point** Potential customers will be dissuaded from purchasing a technologically immature product with a high cost of failure. Furthermore, even if you find buyers for an untried technology,
they could be hurt badly by investing large sums in something that
might bomb out. Wait until the technology is perfected to introduce
it at this level.

C Develop medium-sized desalinators to supply fresh water in Third
World countries that are in dire need of it?

▶ **1 point** You are to be applauded for your humanitarian instincts, but your financial instincts leave something to be desired.
While the Third World could definitely benefit from your process,
can it afford to purchase something with precious funds that runs
the risk of failure? Probably not. Make a few million first, make the
process foolproof, and then form a foundation that will assist Third
World countries.

Score _____   **Running Score for Part III** _____

━━━━━━━━━━━━━━━━━━━━━━━━━━━━▶ **THE BOTTOM LINE**

Buyers who are likely to be damaged financially by the failure of a new
product will be slower to respond to innovation. Until automobiles
became reliable, cabdrivers continued to stick with horse-drawn car-
riages.

Scenario #65
Solar Power

There was a period when the sun never set on the British Empire, and it is very possible that the sun will never set on your financial empire, now that your company has developed a solar cell that is more than competitive with other sources of electricity. Best of all, you don't use any expensive components, just ultrapure single-crystal silicon, which is essentially made from sand. You name it, these little honeys can power it. Your company has already made the front pages of the *Wall Street Journal,* and has dominated the financial news for the last few days. As the company's resident curmudgeon, it is your duty to look for potential dark clouds in order to make sure that the sun will continue to shine. Are you most concerned about

▶ **A**

The need to make sure that your solar cells fit the specifications for products that might use them?

or

▶ **B**

Buyers who might hold back, waiting for second- and third-generation improvements?

or

▶ **C**

The need to make sure that you have access to ultrapure, single-crystal silicon to manufacture your solar cells?

➡️

Solutions #65: **Solar Power**

A The need to make sure that your solar cells fit the specifications for products that might use them?

▶ **I point** This is certainly something to think about, but any concern about this is relatively minor. Even if other products require cells designed to other specifications, if your development is truly spectacular, the next generation of products will be designed to use whatever you produce. There will even be industries that will manufacture converters to use your cells.

B Buyers who might hold back, waiting for second- and third-generation improvements?

▶ **0 points** Undoubtedly some buyers will hold back for this reason, but there will be buyers who will immediately benefit from your cells and will jump feetfirst into first-generation technology. As the technology and reliability improve, you will later attract the buyers to the second- and third-generation products.

C The need to make sure that you have access to ultrapure, single-crystal silicon to manufacture your solar cells?

▶ **5 points** Even though the foundation of your business is built on sand, you'd better make sure there is enough of it. It is frustrating to be able to spin gold out of straw, as your cells promise to do, and then discover that you can't obtain any straw! Insure yourself against the large risks and move ahead. The small problems can be resolved as you go.

Score _____   **Running Score for Part III** _____

━━━━━━━━━━━━━━━━━━▶ **THE BOTTOM LINE**

Any enterprise must be constantly on the lookout to make sure that it is never without supplies. As Napoleon said, an army travels on its stomach.

Scenario #66

Cleaning Up

Although there have been no developments in the vacuum cleaner industry for twenty years, and some say the market is saturated, your firm has been cleaning up. You were in on the ground floor, have seen the industry weather some tough times, and have emerged to make a consistent, tidy profit. However, there is no reason to let down your guard because the industry as a whole is no longer expanding, and you are looking at possible ways to improve your profit picture. On the bad side: there are not many households that do not have vacuum cleaners. But on the good side: the Second Law of Thermodynamics guarantees that clean things will continually get dirty. Considering the state of the industry, do you feel you should

▶ **A**

Concentrate on discovering the potential weak points of your competitors in order to improve your market share?

or

▶ **B**

Figure that the industry needs a kick in the pants and invest in R & D in order to be first with the breakthrough?

or

▶ **C**

Strive for a "leaner and meaner" posture by concentrating on making sure that the executives are attuned to cost control rather than growth and expansion?

⟶

Solutions #66: **Cleaning Up**

A Concentrate on discovering the potential weak points of your competitors in order to improve your market share?

▶ **5 points**   When an industry is growing, the good times enable all the firms in the industry to prosper, but those times are in
the past for this particular market. Mature industries usually reward
strategies based on improving market share, and this represents your
best offensive move and your best chance at a substantial increase
in profits.

B Figure that the industry needs a kick in the pants and invest in R & D
in order to be first with the breakthrough?

▶ **I point**   Money invested in R & D is not necessarily money
thrown down the drain. You could get lucky and discover voice-
activated vacuum cleaners, or some such development, and jump off
to an early lead. All things considered, though, this should be your
lowest priority.

C Strive for a "leaner and meaner" posture by concentrating on making
sure that the executives are attuned to cost control rather than
growth and expansion?

▶ **5 points**   It never hurts to try to improve the bottom-line
picture through such commonsense measures as cost control, and
this is even more important in a mature industry than in an expanding one, where growth can compensate for sloppiness. Mature
industries usually reward intelligent defensive moves, and this is the
best one available. Moreover, lowered costs can often lead to increased market share.

Score _____   **Running Score for Part III** _____

━━━━━━━━━━━━━━━━━━━➤ **THE BOTTOM LINE**

In a mature industry that is unlikely to undergo much expansion, acquiring an increased market share is the name of the game. A mature
stallion constantly tries to increase the size of his herd at the expense
of his rivals.

Scenario #67

Surf City

You're worried about one of the classic executive dilemmas; your regional managers may be over the hill. True, most of them are still on the low side of forty, but the surfboard game is not the same as it was when they "told the teacher they're surfin', surfin' U.S.A." They're still doing a good job, but it isn't clear that their fingers are on the pulse of what's happening now. The odd thing is that the surfboard industry is currently expanding, as a new generation starts to hang ten and shoot the curl. Is it preferable to

▶ **A**

Stay with what you've got, as it seems to be working out okay, but put any expansion plans on the back burner?

or

▶ **B**

Hire some new managers (preferably belonging to today's generation) to set the direction for future expansion?

or

▶ **C**

Trust to the experience of your current managers and let them plan for the future expansion of your company?

⟶

Solutions #67: **Surf City**

A Stay with what you've got, as it seems to be working out okay, but put any expansion plans on the back burner?

▶ **2 points**   A little on the stodgy side, perhaps, but it's a decision that will not only keep you in the black but is unlikely to generate a tidal wave of red ink. Let everybody call you a fuddy-duddy, but you will laugh all the way to the bank. You may not drive away in a Rolls, but you'll be making regular deposits.

B Hire some new managers (preferably belonging to today's generation) to set the direction for future expansion?

▶ **5 points**   You are in an industry that is known for its trendiness, and if you want to set a course for the future, it's probably best to set sail with those who are most likely to be on top of things. This is the type of decision that often is extremely difficult to make, as those at the top level of management are likely to belong to the old guard and are not in sympathy with new trends. It is also possible to set up a new products division with new management and use the current operations as a cash cow.

C Trust to the experience of your current managers and let them plan for the future expansion of your company?

▶ **0 points**   This is the worst of the available decisions but one that is made far more often than top level managers care to admit. In some industries, experience in making decisions pays dividends; the learning curve is a major factor in success. However, it is sad but true that pioneers can lose touch; just look at Steven Jobs in microcomputers or Nolan Bushnell in video games.

Score _____   **Running Score for Part III** _____

━━━━━━━━━━━━━━━━━━━━━━━━━━━▶ **THE BOTTOM LINE**

It is sometimes possible to provide for low-risk growth by starting "maverick operations," small, separate entrepreneurial divisions in promising areas. Lockheed's famous Skunk Works ended up smelling like a rose.

Scenario #68

Close Calculation

While looking over the latest financial reports of your hand calculator company, you can't help but think wistfully back to the good old days when you would manufacture a calculator that could add, subtract, multiply, and divide for $15, sell it for $90, and have them lining up to place orders. Now you make 'em for $1, sell them to retailers for $2, and hope that they will sell for $5. All this is having a deleterious effect on your company's fortunes, and it is up to you to take steps to brighten the profit picture. You are going to have to recognize that the hand calculator business is no longer in a period of rapid expansion, and take appropriate measures. Should you

▶ **A**

Invest in research to find additional types of hand calculators that might add to your profits?

   or

▶ **B**

Take a hard look at your product line and eliminate those calculators that are clearly putting in a subpar performance?

   or

▶ **C**

Add extra manufacturing capacity in order to increase your profit by increasing your volume?

⟶

Solutions #68: **Close Calculation**

A Invest in research to find additional types of hand calculators that might add to your profits?

▶ **1 point**   This would certainly be an excellent idea in a growing market, but in a market that has settled down, it isn't such a good one. While the odds are that you won't spend yourself into the poorhouse, the odds are against your discovering a winner. Making a move such as this indicates that you have not acknowledged that the industry has stopped growing.

B Take a hard look at your product line and eliminate those calculators that are clearly putting in a subpar performance?

▶ **5 points**   The time has come to focus on your product mix and take a good, hard look at exactly where both your profits and your losses are coming from. When an industry matures, a good way to improve the overall profit picture is by stopping the sources of red ink. This move is often difficult to make, as it requires a realistic assessment of a situation in which the outlook is no longer euphoric.

C Add extra manufacturing capacity in order to increase your profit by increasing your volume?

▶ **−1 point**   There is a possibility that a move like this might help alleviate a temporarily bleak picture, but in the long run, it rates to be counterproductive. If you don't sell what you thought you would sell, you're already in trouble, and if you do, you are liable to intensify competition in the industry, which will hurt matters in the long run. Additional research and added production capacity are inappropriate in a mature industry, which is the environment for cutting costs and milking any available cash cows.

Score _____   **Running Score for Part III** _____

➡ **THE BOTTOM LINE**

When an industry is no longer expanding, it is especially important to stop the bleeding by eliminating sources of loss. When a plant is no longer growing, the dead portions must be pruned so that energy is not uselessly diverted; then harvest the fruit before the plant dies.

Scenario #69

Match Point

There was a time when a tennis tournament appeared on television almost every week, and orders were backed up for almost a year from the Beverly Hills set, each wanting you to build a tennis court on his or her property. Well, Beverly Hills is almost saturated with tennis courts now, your backlog is almost nonexistent, and you're even installing tennis courts for the *nouveau riche* who have settled in the San Fernando Valley or Orange County. The truth is that the tennis boom seems to have peaked, and where you couldn't keep up with orders before, you're now having to work harder to find them. Nonetheless, it might still be possible for you to make a comfortable profit if you

▶ **A**

Intensify your marketing efforts to build more tennis courts, even build them some distance away from your base of operations.

   or

▶ **B**

Realize that what you essentially do is put down slabs of concrete and paint lines on them, and go into related areas such as building playgrounds with basketball courts marked on them.

   or

▶ **C**

Increase the services associated with building your tennis courts, build cabanas, and supply maintenance services.

⟶

Solutions #69: **Match Point**

A   Intensify your marketing efforts to build more tennis courts, even build them some distance away from your base of operations.

▶ **I point**   This might temporarily up the number of orders you receive. However, you face the same difficulties that an advancing army does; the further it moves from its base of supply, the harder it is to keep the momentum going. In addition, the frantic hustle for new buyers is less likely to succeed in an industry that is no longer in the growth phase.

B   Realize that what you essentially do is put down slabs of concrete and paint lines on them, and go into related areas such as building playgrounds with basketball courts marked on them.

▶ **–I point**   If nobody else were doing this, it would be an extremely wise move. However, nearly every schoolyard and every municipality already has playgrounds; do you think the stork brought them? In general, trying to play somebody else's game relinquishes the home court advantage.

C   Increase the services associated with building your tennis courts, build cabanas, and supply maintenance services.

▶ **5 points**   There is no guarantee associated with this, but at least you would be sticking with what you do best and attempting to increase the marginal profitability of each tennis court you build by making incremental sales to existing customers. In a mature industry, this is often the best strategy. Higher margins on the peripheral items can enhance eroding margins on the basic business.

Score _____   **Running Score for Part III** _____

━━━━━━━━━━━━━━━━━━━━━━━━━━━━━━▶ **THE BOTTOM LINE**

Mature industries often feature adding value and services to the product line rather than searching for additional customers. A pitcher who is losing his or her fastball has to acquire a repertoire of off-speed pitches.

Scenario #70

Dirty Pool

As your airliner came in for a landing at Los Angeles Airport, you couldn't help but notice the incredibly large number of houses that had swimming pools. As the sales manager of a large manufacturer of swimming pools, this was a cause for satisfaction; clearly, you had done a good job. All of a sudden, though, you realized that it was also a cause for concern. It might well be possible to put two cars in every garage, or a TV set in every room in the house, but it would probably be impossible to put two swimming pools on a given lot. Sooner or later, the market is probably going to take a dive, and your personal future might be in some jeopardy. Should you

▶ **A**

Continue to hold on to your comfortably secure position at your current company, even though you realize that the water will probably get choppy in a few years?

or

▶ **B**

Accept an offer with a rival swimming pool builder at a higher salary?

or

▶ **C**

Try to find another position in an industry that still has time to catch the wave?

⟶

Solutions #70: **Dirty Pool**

A Continue to hold on to your comfortably secure position at your current company, even though you realize that the water will probably get choppy in a few years?

▶ **1 point**   This is not necessarily a bad choice, as it depends to some extent on your goals and aspirations. Many businesses are cyclical; they do well, they go through periods where they do relatively poorly, and then they do well again. If you are prepared to stick with a secure position, reduce your expectations for advancement, and ride out the rough water later, this might well be the best choice.

B Accept an offer with a rival swimming pool builder at a higher salary?

▶ **0 points**   You are still going to find yourself in trouble later on, but this time you will have traded long-term security for short-term profits. As a result, you may find that you are expendable when the tide turns.

C Try to find another position in an industry that still has time to catch the wave?

▶ **5 points**   Just as every stock purchaser wants to get in while the market is still going up, every salesperson would like to be selling something that is in increasing demand. Nice work if you can get it, and if you see an opportunity to switch, now is probably a good time to do so.

Score _____   **Running Score for Part III** _____

━━━━━━━━━━━━━━━━━━━━━━━━▶ **THE BOTTOM LINE**

Although an individual company may be doing well, the industry may be about to fall on hard times. The wise rat deserts the ship before it sinks.

Scenario #71

Fast Forward

You've been manufacturing videocassette recorders since the first primitive models came on the market. Remember those dinosaurs? They could record a single two-hour program, cost $1,500, and represented the latest in high tech. Well, the market for videocassette recorders has certainly stabilized. It's unlikely that the market will ever disappear, but the price has fallen to about $250 for a videocassette recorder that will do everything but make your breakfast. Competition has intensified, and profit margins have been squeezed, and you are going to have to do something to help your company maintain its profitability. Does your best chance lie with

▶ **A**

Improving your manufacturing methods and perhaps cutting down on bureaucratic overhead?

or

▶ **B**

Expanding your product line to include even glitzier videocassette recorders that will make your breakfast?

or

▶ **C**

Engaging in an aggressive advertising campaign with an eye to capturing a greater share of the market?

⟶

Solutions #71: **Fast Forward**

A Improving your manufacturing methods and perhaps cutting down on bureaucratic overhead?

▶ **5 points** It's not glamorous, it's not high tech, and it's not NOW, but it's the most advisable thing to do in a mature industry. In a period of rapid growth, mistakes in efficiency are covered up by industry expansion. When the industry is no longer expanding, individual firms must become more efficient.

B Expanding your product line to include even glitzier videocassette recorders that will make your breakfast?

▶ **0 points** Although you might get lucky and open new areas of a market that essentially seems closed, additional expenditures must be given a long, hard look in an industry that is no longer growing. It is sometimes difficult to accept the fact that an industry is no longer growing and that the public's desire for newer, glitzier gadgets has peaked out, and this is a trap into which many firms regrettably fall. Don't try to transform a mature product, for which demand is stable, into a growth industry.

C Engaging in an aggressive advertising campaign with an eye to capturing a greater share of the market?

▶ **2 points** On the good side: you have recognized that this is no longer a growth game but a market share game, and that one road to increased profitability lies in expanding your market share. An important way to improve company performance in a mature industry is to increase market share. However, an aggressive advertising campaign might simply promote industry warfare, and if this degenerates into price cutting, everyone will be the loser.

Score _____   **Running Score for Part III** _____

━━━━━━━━━━━━━━━━━━━━━━━━━━━━▶ **THE BOTTOM LINE**

Reduce the overhead and avoid new capital expenditures to keep the "cash cow" profitable. Why spread fertilizer today if you're going to harvest the crop tomorrow?

Scenario #72

Watch Out!

When you began construction of the new, efficient plant to manufacture top-of-the-line digital watches, it seemed like a good idea. Although your company was small, both it and the industry seemed to be making giant strides. You had come to expect that the public would simply keep buying any new development in the industry; all you had to do was come up with more bells and whistles. Unfortunately, your firm's projections indicate that this is no longer the case. Incredible though it may seem, the public is actually becoming reactionary, and a trend is setting in to buy watches in which time is told by pointers on a circular dial; these pointers, or so you are told, are called "hands." What to do with that new plant? Should you

▶ **A**

Use the plant, as you originally intended, to manufacture more top-of-the-line, glitzier digital watches?

   or

▶ **B**

Invest in a research program to find ways in which the plant can be modified to produce other products using digital technology?

   or

▶ **C**

Sell the plant while it still has value and there is a demand for it?

⟶

Solutions #72: **Watch Out!**

A Use the plant, as you originally intended, to manufacture more top-of-the-line, glitzier digital watches?

▶ **–2 points**   Unfortunately, focusing on utilization of excess capacity as a dominant variable is one of the most common traps in the game when demand falters. The actual result of doing so is liable to be counterproductive. Rather than generating watches that an eager public is willing to buy, you are more likely to be creating a larger supply, which will drive prices and profits inexorably downward.

B Invest in a research program to find ways in which the plant can be modified to produce other products using digital technology?

▶ **2 points**   You are a small company and would be competing with larger, more established firms in the new area, which runs high risks unless you see an unusual niche. This is the classic poker trap of paying money to draw to an inside straight, when a straight might not be good enough to take the pot. On the other hand, you could have a winner, and it is better than saturating the market with more digital watches.

C Sell the plant while it still has value and there is a demand for it?

▶ **5 points**   There are times when others can make better use of your assets than you can. As they say in professional sports, a good trade is one that helps both teams. Ideally, you would like to sell the plant to some firm from outside the industry, which has an established competitive position in the manufacture of digital coffeepots, or some such item. Such a firm can probably better utilize your efficient plant processes and developed skills.

Score _____   **Running Score for Part III** _____

━━━━━━━━━━━━━━━━━━━━━━━━━━━━▶ **THE BOTTOM LINE**

Overhanging excess capacity in a mature industry can be an albatross around the necks of both the corporation and the industry. When there is little food, the smallest bird in the nest goes hungry so that the others may survive.

Scenario #73

Tough Sledding

The time is sometime in the early twenty-first century. For more than one hundred years, the firm that you head has been the world's leading manufacturer of recreational winter sports items such as skis and sleds. Now, however, you must face up to a problem you never in your wildest dreams imagined: the greenhouse effect. The rising oceans are lapping at the streets of downtown New York City, and only Alaska, Canada, and points above the Arctic Circle are still experiencing normal winter conditions. Still, the demand for your sleds is strong in cold climes, although other, smaller sled manufacturers are falling by the wayside. Projections show that, by the year 2300, they'll be surfing in Nome in December. Should you

▶ **A**

Switch from skis and sleds to surfboards and swimming equipment as soon as possible?

or

▶ **B**

Take advantage of the current demise of your competitors by concentrating on those areas in which winter temperatures are low and demand for skis and sleds is high?

or

▶ **C**

Gradually phase out of manufacturing winter sports equipment, and retool to make water skis?

$\longrightarrow$

Solutions #73: **Tough Sledding**

A Switch from skis and sleds to surfboards and swimming equipment as
   soon as possible?

▶ **–2 points**   Although the situation is not good, there is no
need for immediate panic. You will probably want to contemplate
such a move eventually, but why the rush? If New York were under-
water, rather than merely a little damp, you might consider this, but
geologic catastrophes fortunately occur on a relatively slow scale.
Act in haste, repent at leisure.

B Take advantage of the current demise of your competitors by concentrating on those areas in which winter temperatures are low and demand for skis and sleds is high?

▶ **5 points**   The market can still be exited profitably, as they
are still enjoying winter sports in many areas, and so you should
take advantage of your leadership of the industry and the weakness
of your competitors to assume a dominant role. Profits can still be
made, and you are in excellent position to emerge with the lion's
share. A leadership strategy in a declining industry can enable the
strong to prosper while the weak die off.

C Phase out of manufacturing winter sports equipment over the next
   few years, and retool to make water skis?

▶ **2 points**   This is a reasonable approach, but you don't have
to hit the panic button quite so soon. Nonetheless, it is a good idea
to start looking for ways to utilize your assets in a new environment.

Score _____   **Running Score for Part III** _____

━━━━━━━━━━━━━━━━━━━━━━━━━━▶ **THE BOTTOM LINE**

In a declining industry, one possible strategy is to seize leadership. It
is easiest to bring off a coup when the government is in chaos.

Scenario #74

Cold Turkey

You have had a profitable thing going for many years, shipping refrigerated poultry from poultry farms to restaurants. Your massive advertising campaign has made the slogan "Our Trucks + Your Ducks = Big Bucks" a household phrase. However, all good things must come to an end, and the refrigerated poultry-shipping business has clearly seen better days. It's time to get out, but you want to stage a calm, orderly retreat, rather than a precipitous flight. There are several possible moves you can make, which will add to your bottom line, and you want to be certain to execute these moves in the proper order. Should you first

▶ **A**

Cut down on advertising, figuring that since everyone knows who you are, you can save a couple of bucks?

or

▶ **B**

Save maintenance costs by overhauling your delivery fleet less frequently?

or

▶ **C**

Institute a round of price hikes, figuring that you will make up your volume loss by greater profits per haul, and can then sell off your excess inventory slowly?

$\longrightarrow$

Solutions #74: **Cold Turkey**

A Cut down on advertising, figuring that since everyone knows who you are, you can save a couple of bucks?

▶ **5 points**　You probably have one of the world's more memorable slogans, and it will be some time before anyone who needs to ship refrigerated poultry will forget "Our Trucks + Your Ducks = Big Bucks." Besides, you can always paint it on your trucks, if it isn't there already. A harvest strategy maximizes cash flow from a company in a declining industry.

B Save maintenance costs by overhauling your delivery fleet less frequently?

▶ **–1 point**　Here's a classic example of being penny-wise but pound-foolish. If you don't overhaul your delivery fleet sufficiently often, you may find the refrigeration cutting out during the middle of a long haul. Not only will you lose out by failing to make your deliveries, the aroma from insufficiently refrigerated poultry is unforgettable. If your intention is to pursue a harvest strategy, you might consider gradually selling off your equipment.

C Institute a round of price hikes, figuring that you will make up your volume loss by greater profits per haul, and can then sell off your excess inventory slowly?

▶ **1 point**　Not a bad idea, assuming that your price hikes only chase off a few of your customers. But what if you lose a whole bunch? Certainly, you can restore the original prices, but by then you will have lost some customers anyway.

Score _____　　　　　　　**Running Score for Part III** _____

━━━━━━━━━━━━━━━━━━━━━━━━━━▶ **THE BOTTOM LINE**

A harvest strategy is suitable for a company in a declining industry, as it maximizes cash flow. There is a time to plant, a time to grow, and a time to bring in the sheaves.

Scenario #75

Trouble Brewing

It's hard for you, as the head of a medium-sized distillery selling to customers in the good old U.S.A., to remain in good spirits these days. Your stockholders have plenty to gripe about as, although no one believes that the liquor industry will dry up, it's hard to quell the rumors that your industry is about to enter a period of significant decline, which may last for a number of years. Antidrug crusaders are starting to turn their attention to alcohol as the nation's number one drug of choice. There has been a great deal of publicity given to the fact that drunk drivers kill more people annually than AIDS. The international market is doing reasonably well, but things are looking grim on the home front; the Surgeon General is even thinking about requiring you to place a warning on each bottle. Even though your industry has weathered storms before, this looks like the worst one since Prohibition. There are several options available, so should you

▶ **A**

Take advantage of the pullout of several other small distillers to buy their equipment and move towards a leadership role in the domestic market?

or

▶ **B**

Unload the firm's assets, lock, stock, and barrel, to a diversified conglomerate that has made a reasonable offer?

or

▶ **C**

Attempt to pull out of the market slowly by gradually selling off your distilleries on a regional basis?

→

Solutions #75: **Trouble Brewing**

A Take advantage of the pullout of several other small distillers to buy their equipment and move towards a leadership role in the domestic market?

▶ **–2 points** There are times when the situation requires the courage and optimism of a Washington at Valley Forge, or a Churchill during the London Blitz. This is most emphatically *not* one of those times. Your competitors, who are larger, more diversified, and international in scope, can weather the storm better than you can. Any aggressive action by you will bring disastrous retaliation.

B Unload the firm's assets, lock, stock, and barrel, to a diversified conglomerate that has made a reasonable offer?

▶ **5 points** Call them on the phone *right now*, and accept their offer. Because you are a single-line firm, you will get badly hurt by a decline in domestic sales; whereas a diversified conglomerate is in a much better position to ride it out. In this case you know why someone else can do better with your assets than you can, but you can't duplicate his or her capability.

C Attempt to pull out of the market slowly by gradually selling off your distilleries on a regional basis?

▶ **0 points** While this plan preserves the option of getting back into the game if the mood of the country changes, it looks like the axe is going to fall, and you want to get your head off the chopping block as soon as possible. Remember, most options expire worthless.

Score _____   **Running Score for Part III** _____

━━━━━━━━━━━━━━━━━━━━━━━▶ **THE BOTTOM LINE**

Divestment may be an expedient strategy in a declining industry. When you are trapped in a burning building, get out!

Scenario #76

The Whole Enchilada

You used to be able to sell tacos in Tacoma, tamales in Tamalpais, and burritos in Burlington, but unfortunately the taste of the fickle American public has swung away from Mexican food. While there are still customers everywhere, and the profit picture is still *muy bueno* in Texas and the Southwest, sales are slipping in most other places, which places your nationwide chain of Mexican restaurants in some jeopardy. As a result, you have some important decision making to do, and pronto. You have no desire to find yourself peddling enchiladas to a quiche-eating public. Does your best chance lie with

▶ **A**

Putting the whole enterprise up for sale, thereby limiting your losses?

or

▶ **B**

Hanging on to your profitable operations in Texas and the Southwest, while gradually trying to unload your other outlets?

or

▶ **C**

Trying to guess the next food trend of the American public and redesigning your restaurants and menus accordingly?

⟶

Solutions #76: **The Whole Enchilada**

A Putting the whole enterprise up for sale, thereby limiting your losses?

▶ **0 points** Desperation moves are only advisable in desperate situations, and this does not seem to be the case. In general, there are only two times when a wholesale bailout is advisable: in a rising market, when everybody wants to buy what you are selling, and when there is a gun to your head and you have no other choice. This just doesn't fit either scenario.

B Hanging on to your profitable operations in Texas and the Southwest, while gradually trying to unload your other outlets?

▶ **5 points** While nobody likes to find himself or herself in a deteriorating situation, it is made more tolerable when there is a comfortable niche into which you can retreat while gradually disinvesting. In addition, by maintaining a base you can get back into the game later if the situation warrants.

C Trying to guess the next food trend of the American public and redesigning your restaurants and menus accordingly?

▶ **−2 points** You are getting away from your strength, which is preparing and selling Mexican food, and gambling on your ability to predict future trends. There are a lot of ways for you to be wrong and cost yourself even more money, and only one way for you to be right. The odds are strongly against it.

Score _____   **Running Score for Part III** _____

➡ **THE BOTTOM LINE**

In a declining industry, a niche strategy involves locating a segment of the industry, which will maintain both stable return and high demand. When his or her stake is disappearing, a poker player stays in the pot only with a good hand.

Scenario #77

Cash Cow

Several years ago the conglomerate of which you are the head went into a feeding frenzy, during which it bought up a lot of companies doing an assortment of things. On reviewing this year's balance sheet, you were amazed to see that the small frozen yogurt company that was one of your acquisitions has become the country's largest frozen yogurt chain and is making money hand over fist! However, it's win a few, lose a few; some of the other acquisitions that your conglomerate made aren't doing quite so well. You are a little worried that, although many people are putting toppings on their frozen yogurt, the market for frozen yogurt may be doing some topping of its own. Meanwhile, you have an excess of money from your yogurt operations, and what are you going to do with it? Should you

▶ **A**

Stick with a good thing and plow the money from selling frozen yogurt back into more frozen yogurt?

or

▶ **B**

Use the money to expand capacity in one of your acquisitions that has a small share of a fast-growing market?

or

▶ **C**

Use the money to improve the picture of one of your acquisitions that is not doing so well?

➡

Solutions #77: **Cash Cow**

A Stick with a good thing and plow the money from selling frozen yogurt back into more frozen yogurt?

▶ **0 points**   On the surface, it's certainly appealing to continue to back a winner. However, capacity expansion in an industry that appears to have topped out is fraught with peril; if you end up producing too much frozen yogurt at a time when the American taste swings back to ice cream, you may end up in the ignominious position of having turned a winner into a loser. More likely, since the demand has topped out, any expansion on your part can lead to overcapacity, price cuts, and reduced profitability, unless you can somehow take market share away from your competitors.

B Use the money to expand capacity in one of your acquisitions that has a small share of a fast-growing market?

▶ **5 points**   The classic move in this situation is to milk the money that the cash cow is producing, and use it to fund capacity expansion in a fast-growing industry. While there is very rarely a sure thing in the capacity expansion game, it is a lot easier to expand capacity into an increasing demand than into a steady or possibly declining one.

C Use the money to improve the picture of one of your acquisitions that is not doing so well?

▶ **−2 points**   One of the classic investment traps in any integrated business entity is to try to help out the weak sister when there is no potential from here. Capital and expertise previously invested are sunk costs and therefore irrelevant.

Score _____   **Running Score for Part III** _____

━━━━━━━━━━━━━━━━━━━━━━━━━━━━▶ **THE BOTTOM LINE**

The major portion of expansion capital, as well as the best management people in the company, should be focused on the most promising areas, as the company's growth is not going to come from the problem areas and losing divisions. It does no good to beat a dead horse.

8

Strategies for International Markets

THE ISSUES

One of the dominant forces at work today is the globalization of markets. It is not unusual to read of companies that produce a product in Switzerland, assemble it in West Germany, and market it through an Irish firm. Such behavior means that the prices of assets in world markets are going to reflect the efficiency we have come to take for granted in the United States. There is no question that we are living in a world in which the development of global strategies for manufacturing and marketing will play an increasingly important role in determining competitive success.

As a result, not only must firms be aware of the national industrial environment, they must be aware of the international industrial environment as well. Consider, for instance, the second of the three questions that a firm addresses, the nature of the competition. In many industries, consideration of the competition from international sources is a dominant variable that must be considered. As American automobile firms learned to their sorrow in the late 1960s and early 1970s, neglecting international competition can be very costly, even fatal.

The central issues for firms competing in international markets revolve around the strategic advantages and disadvantages of competing worldwide, either with a full line of products or with a particular segment of products, as opposed to competing in a few national markets where favorable marketing niches can be found. The industry itself may be global in nature, but the individual company's position within the industry may be local, national, limited international, or truly worldwide in scope.

Each company's strategy is determined not only by its own position but also by the position of its rivals. It is difficult, for instance, to be a low-cost producer if one's competitors are global companies, with access to advantages that a smaller firm cannot hope to achieve. However, the global giant will have difficulty competing in markets where local idiosyncrasies strongly influence consumer preferences.

No company can afford to be oblivious to the possibilities afforded by the existence of global commerce. Not only will local preferences influence local markets, but local conditions may render products or services highly profitable in some areas, marginally profitable in others, and totally infeasible in still others.

Modes of Entry; Rewards and Risks

All international giants were fledgling international enterprises at one stage of their existence, and every company that contemplates the possibility of moving beyond its national boundaries must investigate the different ways of doing so. Three important ways of entering the international market are via licensing agreements, export, and direct foreign investment. Each of these represents a different combination of reward and risk, and companies in different situations will find that their choice of mode of entry will be largely influenced by their assessment of the potential rewards and risks.

Of the above three modes of entry, licensing agreements represent the mode with the least risk. When a company licenses a product or process, an institution in the other country pays for the rights to the product or process. While direct risks, such as loss of capital, associated with this mode are usually small, indirect risks, such as loss of proprietary information, can be large. Additionally, with respect to these three approaches, the inflexible relation between reward and risk (the smaller the risk, the smaller the reward) may well limit the company's ability to capitalize on its product.

Exporting to foreign markets assumes a larger risk. In particular, the exporting company usually assumes much of the marketing risk, which may be substantial. In exchange for this, the exporting company retains control of the product or process. This may entail a substantially larger reward.

Direct foreign investment, in which the company leases or purchases facilities in another country, is yet a third mode of entry. Riskier than licensing, there may well be substantial advantages to this approach, as it may be possible to achieve substantial savings in labor or materials, to say nothing of shipping costs. Various mobility barriers, such as local legislation, sometimes make this mode of entry the only feasible one.

Obstacles

Local legislation can be a significant obstacle to the creation of a truly global strategy. Most of the markets that are of interest to industry exist in economies that are nominally free, but are in reality fettered by a government whose legislative policy is shaped by people who work in jobs that are often threatened by more efficient production in another part of the world. Given the choice between supplying better products at a more competitive price for the majority of its citizens, or protecting the jobs of a minority, a government often opts for the latter course. This is not surprising, since an individual who is harmed by governmental action is more likely to take umbrage than one who is merely denied benefits through governmental inaction.

Unique Risks Associated with a Global Strategy

Certain unique risks must be considered in formulating a global strategy. Although the industry environment in the United States is obviously subject to rapid and sudden changes, the overall political climate is relatively stable. Investing in a country, such as China, may well offer substantial rewards in opening up huge, untapped markets, but the fact that the political climate can be subject to extreme instability presents an added element of risk. Changes of government can lead to nationalization of an industry, and uncompensated loss of the capital invested.

Even when the political climate is relatively stable, devaluation or revaluation of currency, as well as currency restrictions, can have a profound effect on bottom-line performance.

Despite these hazards, the world has already moved toward a global economy, which is accompanied by globally efficient markets. In the past, the global environment has been of concern only to multinational corporations, or import–export firms taking advantage of local conditions. In the future the global environment will be of increasing importance to more firms in a greater number of industries.

Scenario #78
Designer Genes

You got into the designer gene game fairly early, and now your genetic engineering company is one of the most respected in the country. Of special interest are your friendly bacteria, which turn out insulin without the necessity of slaughtering large numbers of livestock. It has been a profitable business in the United States, and you want to dip your toes into the international market, which does not seem quite as sold on genetic engineering as does the United States, without taking an undue amount of risk. You have recently started negotiations with a large pharmaceutical firm and are wondering what your best approach is. Should you

▶ **A**

Invest directly in manufacturing facilities in Switzerland, manufacture the insulin, and have them distribute it?

or

▶ **B**

Grant them a license to manufacture the insulin using your process?

or

▶ **C**

Manufacture the insulin in the United States, and export it for sale?

→

Solutions #78: **Designer Genes**

A Invest directly in manufacturing facilities in Switzerland, manufacture the insulin, and have them distribute it?

▶ **–1 point**   This is high-stakes poker. Not only are you assuming a huge risk in building the facilities, you are not sure whether the product will ever be successful in foreign markets.

B Grant them a license to manufacture the insulin using your process?

▶ **5 points**   This is the time to minimize your risk. You are guaranteed money in the bank, no matter what happens on the other side of the Atlantic, and as a first international venture it's hard to turn down a sure thing. You will not gain hands-on experience marketing or manufacturing in Switzerland, but you will acquire valuable information without risk. Licensing is an excellent way to make a profit from proprietary product technology, and enables you enter a global environment, in which the learning curve is steep, in a comfortable fashion.

C Manufacture the insulin in the United States, and export it for sale?

▶ **2 points**   A reasonable halfway move. It is slightly riskier than licensing, for you are running the risk that for one reason or another you may be unable to bring it to market. However, if you work out the regulatory and legal details, as well as other questions, such as who controls the marketing and who pays shipping, you'll end up with a larger profit because you control the supply. In any case, the international experience you gain will serve you well in the future.

Score _____   **Running Score for Part III** _____

═══════════════════════════════════════▶ **THE BOTTOM LINE**

Although licensing is probably the least lucrative of possible ways to enter the global market, it is the least risky. If you suspect that the water may be unpleasantly cold, it is advisable to dip your toes in before taking the plunge.

Scenario #79

Nontrivial Pursuit

Every so often a venture works so well, it's almost scary. A few years ago you came to market with an idea for a board game that took every penny you had, and now it's on the verge of becoming the next Trivial Pursuit. There are few pleasures in life to compare with marketing a square of cardboard, some plastic markers, and a page or so of printed instructions for $40; it's almost like counterfeiting money. Foreign investors are now beating down your door, literally begging for an opportunity to market your game in their country. How can you refuse? What you really want to do is maximize your profits, because you know it will be a success from Austria to Zimbabwe. Should you

▶ A

Add some extra manufacturing capacity by building or leasing, run the presses overtime, and export the game?

or

▶ B

Lower the labor cost by buying or renting production facilities in the countries where they will be sold?

or

▶ C

License the game, avoid the hassles of manufacturing elsewhere or boosting capacity, and collect a percentage?

⟶

Solutions #79: **Nontrivial Pursuit**

A Add some extra manufacturing capacity by building or leasing, run the presses overtime, and export the game?

▶ **5 points**   This is a situation in which you want to go for the kill, as there is often a narrow window for such an opportunity. Who knows what people will be doing for fun next year? The best way to do this is to maintain control of the entire procedure. Added labor costs? Shipping costs? Don't worry about it; just boost your prices to cover it and let the overseas sellers do the worrying.

B Lower the labor cost by buying or renting production facilities in the countries where they will be sold?

▶ **1 point**   What labor cost? You're not exactly manufacturing something high tech here, like videocassette recorders or jet fighters. The truth is that these things can probably be manufactured for almost no labor cost, and you will just be inviting extra aggravation by getting involved where you don't need to be.

C License the game, avoid the hassles of manufacturing elsewhere or boosting capacity, and collect a percentage?

▶ **–1 point**   You must like giving away money, because that's what you're doing. Licensing is usually the right move when there is substantial risk that the licensee can lift from the shoulders of the licenser, but that's certainly not the case here.

Score _____   **Running Score for Part III** _____

━━━━━━━━━━━━━━━━━━━━━━━━━━━━━━━━━━➤ **THE BOTTOM LINE**

When there is almost no risk associated with a venture, it is important to maintain as much control of all phases of it as possible. The farmer who sells his produce from a roadside stand gets to keep all of the money.

Scenario #80

Perestroika

The other day you were idly skimming through the paper, when a picture caught your eye that made you sit up straight in your chair. It was one of those classic winter in Moscow pictures that the papers run every year, showing a bunch of women sweeping snow from the streets. You've probably seen a million pictures like it before, but this time a single fact hit home: The women were all wearing babushkas! That's what you do for a living; you make scarves. You got this ingenious idea for a joint American–Soviet project to design and market babushkas. The negotiations hit a stumbling block over the nonconvertibility of the ruble, but you worked that out by agreeing to take your profits in Russian furs, which are highly marketable. The only remaining question is how to produce the scarves. Should you

▶ **A**

Build another mill in the United States, manufacture the babushkas here, and ship them to Russia?

or

▶ **B**

Find a Russian firm to produce the scarves, and license them to do it?

or

▶ **C**

Go the direct foreign investment route by financing a mill in Russia and manufacturing the scarves there?

⟶

Solutions #80: **Perestroika**

A Build another mill in the United States, manufacture the babushkas here, and ship them to Russia?

▶ **-1 point**   Haven't you read those stories which say that the average Russian makes about 80 rubles a week? When you add in the shipping costs, the only people who will be able to afford the scarves will be wives of Politburo members, not exactly a mass market. Additionally, because their currency is nonconvertible they would have to use precious foreign currency to pay for imported goods, making this deal far less plausible.

B Find a Russian firm to produce the scarves, and license them to do it?

▶ **0 points**   What Russian firm? The Russians are heavily into state-sponsored collectivism, and even though capitalism is beginning to make a breakthrough, they don't exactly have Yellow Pages filled with various different clothing manufacturers.

C Go the direct foreign investment route by financing a mill in Russia and manufacturing the scarves there?

▶ **5 points**   You're probably going to have to deal with the government to do this, but the Russian government welcomes the opportunity to produce goods utilizing their labor. There is such a paucity of quality goods in Russia that they will be lining up for the opportunity to buy your babushkas, and so the profit potential of this enterprise is quite good, even if you can't take your profit in hard cash. Doesn't it give you a warm feeling to help solidify Soviet–American relations, and still show a healthy profit in the bargain?

Score _____   **Running Score for Part III** _____

━━━━━━━━━━━━━━━━━━━━━━━━━━━━▶ **THE BOTTOM LINE**

Direct foreign investment is a good way to "go global" when the demand is known to exist and savings can be effected on such items as labor, supplies, transportation, or favorable foreign exchange rates. It is often easier for Mohammed to go to the mountain than for the mountain to come to Mohammed.

Scenario #81

Sporting Proposition

Slazenger has its panther, Izod its crocodile, and Puma its puma, but you can lay claim to the most lethal logo: the insignia of your international sporting goods conglomerate is a hammerhead shark. You have persuaded some of the world's top athletes to endorse your products, and the hammerhead is starting to take a big bite out of the competition, as it shows up throughout the world of sports from Wimbledon to the World Series. A lot of your manufacturing contracts are coming up for renegotiation, and you want to make sure that you can manufacture your products in the most profitable fashion. Considering that you must market your goods in more than fifty countries worldwide, should you

▶ **A**

License the products for manufacture on a national basis?

or

▶ **B**

Attempt to centralize production on an item-by-item basis, manufacturing each item in the area where that particular item can be manufactured most cheaply?

or

▶ **C**

Centralize production on a global basis in order to take advantage of the economies of scale this would generate?

⟶

Solutions #81: **Sporting Proposition**

A License the products for manufacture on a national basis?

▶ **5 points**   Once you realize what the major difficulty will be, the solution stands out. Almost every nation is fiercely protective of its labor force, and many of the basic products you are selling, such as shoes, are manufactured on a worldwide basis. Licensing and allowing for local production is not only the simplest solution, but the least likely to generate friction. Notice once again how important it is to isolate the dominant variable.

B Attempt to centralize production on an item-by-item basis, manufacturing each item in the area where that particular item can be manufactured most cheaply?

▶ **0 points**   In a world that did not feature mobility barriers such as tariffs, this would be the logical solution. Indeed, it is possible to argue that the world would be a lot better off if it adopted a policy that all the world's shoes, for example, should be manufactured where shoe manufacturing can be done most efficiently. Unfortunately, this is not the current state of world trade, and so this solution is not feasible.

C Centralize production on a global basis in order to take advantage of the economies of scale this would generate?

▶ **–2 points**   Just because it may be cheaper to manufacture shoes in Taiwan doesn't mean it will be cheaper to manufacture tennis rackets there, to say nothing of the shipping costs and other mobility barriers.

Score _____   **Running Score for Part III** _____

═══ ➡ **THE BOTTOM LINE**
Mobility barriers can make licensing of products or services the only practical way to globalize an industry. Ideas often encounter less resistance crossing boundaries than do products.

▶ ▶ ▶ ▶ ▶ ▶ ▶ ▶ ▶ ▶ ▶ ▶ # So How Are You Doing?

Let's see whether we can use your score on this section to tell something about you.

If Your Score for Part III Is	You Came to Work by
▶ Over 90	Chauffeur-driven limousine
▶ Between 65 and 89	Imported sports car
▶ Between 40 and 64	Late model subcompact
▶ Between 15 and 39	Public transportation
▶ Less than 15	Hitchhiking

PART IV

Some Major Decisions

9

Vertical Integration

THE ISSUES

Vertical integration is the combination of distinct functions, such as production, distribution, or sales, within the framework of a single business entity.

Depending upon the stage of the production-to-marketing chain occupied by the company desiring to integrate, the integration can be accomplished backwards, towards the production end of the chain, or forward, towards the marketing end. Because the normal flow proceeds from production to marketing, backward integration is sometimes referred to as upstream, and forward integration as downstream.

Costs and Benefits

To the extent that a firm integrates, it becomes responsible for the operating and administrative costs previously borne by the companies with whom the firm had been dealing. The potential advantages of integration must be weighed against the costs assumed by the integrating company.

Among the benefits of vertical integration, whether backward or forward, are possible manufacturing and marketing economies and avoidance of unstable relationships with either buyers or customers in the marketplace. Additionally, a firm may emerge from integration with an enhanced ability to differentiate the product, as would be the case when a firm that uses a particular component purchases the supplier, enabling the firm to tailor the component towards its particular needs.

However, the rewards of integration must be weighed against potential risks. The integrating firm must make a capital commitment and increase its fixed costs. There is also the risk that the integrating firm may dull the competitive edge of its managers because of the assured selling and purchasing relationships that integration guarantees. Assessment of the costs and benefits of either integration or deintegration should be made separately for each major product or service under consideration for forward integration, as well as for each major input under consideration for backward integration. Attention should also be paid to the possible integration of supporting services.

Reducing the Risks

The firm desiring some of the benefits of integration has options available with less risk than those of full integration. A firm can lessen the risks and, concomitantly, the attendant rewards of integration by opting for partial, tapered, integration. Tapered integration is achieved, for example, by producing a portion of a needed component in-house and contracting with outside suppliers for the remainder. The graduated aspect of such a decision can enable a firm selecting this course to evaluate the results and then, if it wishes, decide to integrate to a greater degree, with enhanced prospects for success.

Another available option for the company is quasi integration, in which the firm invests in suppliers or buyers in order to create reliable relationships and reduce some of the uncertainty associated with these functions.

Various actions can be taken in the marketplace in order to cope with, or take advantage of, financial risks, marketing risks, and other strategic risks. For example, an action might be motivated by defensive reasons, where the firm desires to reduce uncertainty by protecting an existing portfolio of commitments against market value changes or actions by others. Motivation for the same transaction might be offensive or speculative, where the firm is trying to exploit an expected change in market value. In both cases, the company's *position* (of commitments) is the same, and the risk is completely determined by that *position* without regard to the motivations for assuming it. Vertical integration, like any marketplace decision, can be viewed from the same perspective. The risk and potential of the integration lies in the firm's *position*, not in the motivation.

The firm contemplating either full or partial vertical integration, whether the primary motivation is offensive or defensive, must evaluate the total *position* it will hold *after* integration. That *position* includes the firm's strategy, structure, and process, as well as its market share, its capacity, and the state of the industry and of the firm's strategic group. It also includes the negotiating power and the probability of adverse market moves by customers and suppliers. Given the firm's *position*, the proposed integration decision should be made on the basis of the change (risk) in the position that would result from the most probable changes in the dominant variables.

Vertical integration is a major decision, and as such must be assessed in the light of the three fundamental questions: the company's identity, the analysis of the competition, and the evaluation of the overall state of the industry. What appears to be an ideal integration move in one environment may prove exceptionally hazardous in another. In a growing industry, for example, integration may be undertaken with some assurance that increasing demand will ameliorate some of the risks. In a mature industry integration may be viewed in a less favorable light, and in a declining one integration may hasten the firm's eventual demise. It would be difficult to imagine a situation in which a firm pursuing a liquidation strategy in a declining industry would even consider integrating.

Global Integration

As world markets move towards increasing globalization, vertical integration becomes increasingly attractive, especially when it can be carried out on an international scale. Whereas the 1960s and 1970s saw the burgeoning of the huge multinational conglomerates, the latter portion of the twentieth century is likely to see substantially more small-scale international vertical integration. Even relatively small firms may find it advantageous to produce in one locale, assemble in another, and direct marketing operations from yet a third.

In a sense international vertical integration is a form of arbitrage, and the advantages that accrue to the integrating (arbitraging) firm can be significant on the global level. Arbitraging results in more efficient markets and frequently leads to greater stability in these markets, as well as a greater variety of goods and services at more competitive prices.

Scenario #82

Preemptive Measure

Near the end of a football game, when the home team is ahead by a point, there are two minutes to go, and the visitors have the ball on their own thirty-yard line, what is the crowd screaming? That's right: "DEE-FENSE!" As a manager of a growing firm that is promising to become a leader in the manufacture of an antiviral drug that is a leading weapon in virtually every hospital's pharmaceutical arsenal, defense against supplier pressure is exactly what you need. Your antiviral drug requires a particular rare mineral, and there is always the danger that the suppliers may decide to pressure you, so you decide on a preemptive strike by integrating backward. However, there are several different supply houses available, and you have to decide whether to

▶ **A**

Opt for tapered integration by purchasing a house that supplies less than your needs, reducing your vulnerability but minimizing your investment and marketing risk.

   or

▶ **B**

Purchase a house that supplies your current needs, guaranteeing that you won't need to dispose of any excess.

   or

▶ **C**

Purchase a house that supplies more than your current needs, requiring a larger capital investment.

⟶

Solutions #82: **Preemptive Measure**

A Opt for tapered integration by purchasing a house that supplies less than your needs, reducing your vulnerability but minimizing your investment and marketing risk.

▶ **2 points** By following this line of action, you will have an assured source for some of your needed input, and the supplier will have assured sales for all its output. Although you will still be dependent on other suppliers, it will be to a lesser degree than now. It is even possible to make a smaller investment with some benefits through quasi integration, investing in a supplier firm to create an alliance without the risk of owning or operating the supplier.

B Purchase a house that supplies your current needs, guaranteeing that you won't need to dispose of any excess?

▶ **3 points** This would be the ideal solution if you were Goldilocks, trying to select the bowl of porridge that is "just right." Because your current needs just match the supply, it would seem that this is the most efficient solution. However, your drug is well entrenched in the pharmacopoeia, and other manufacturers can probably consume any excess supply.

C Purchase a house that supplies more than your current needs, requiring a larger capital investment?

▶ **5 points** If your firm is growing and the drug is so important, it makes sense to take a slight risk by purchasing a larger-than-needed supply. If you continue growing, you'll be glad you did, and even if you don't, there will almost certainly be a market for whatever you can't use. Additionally, there is the added possible advantage of achieving economies of scale. It is important to realize that the greatest risk in the situation in which you find yourself is lack of supply or losing power vis-à-vis your current suppliers and not the uncertainty in selling the output of the purchased supplier.

Score _____

═══════════════════════════════════➤ **THE BOTTOM LINE**

Backward integration can protect a firm from being placed at the mercy of suppliers. The best offense is often a good defense.

Scenario #83

Backward Progress

Your chain of stores selling women's apparel has been steadily expanding over the past few years. You're neither Christian Dior nor K-Mart, but have managed to find a comfortable niche selling a variety of apparel from a variety of manufacturers to a variety of customers. Success always brings thoughts of growth, and your board is considering different vertical integration possibilities. Because you are basically at the end of the supply chain, there are few forward integration options except maybe advertising, and this idea was quickly rejected. However, there are several backward integration options available to you, and you want to be sure to make the right choice. Should you

▶ **A**

Purchase a popular woman's apparel manufacturer, assuring yourself of the exclusive right to sell their line?

or

▶ **B**

Go even further upstream, purchase a factory and work out plans for designing what you will sell?

or

▶ **C**

Skip thoughts of vertical integration and use your energy and capital to expand further?

➡

Solutions #83: **Backward Progress**

A Purchase a popular woman's apparel manufacturer, assuring yourself of the exclusive right to sell their line?

▶ **I point** Although this looks good on the surface, popularity, like fame, is often fleeting. There is a definite danger that the manufacturer may lose touch with the public's taste, and you will then be left with a white elephant. In another, more stable business, this could well be the right move.

B Go even further upstream, purchase a factory and work out plans for designing what you will sell?

▶ **–I point** This is one of those "act in haste, repent at leisure" decisions that are often made and quickly regretted. Your buyers are obviously adept at keeping up with what the public wants, but there is no reason to believe that they can create what the public wants. Successful decisions of this type are the exception rather than the rule.

C Skip thoughts of vertical integration and use your energy and capital to expand further?

▶ **5 points** Sometimes it's hard to accept that you should just do more of what you do well, but that's certainly the case here. Any extracurricular ventures are simply excursions into perilous and uncharted waters. Quite often the greatest success comes to those who are adept at keeping their eyes on the ball.

Score _____   **Running Score for Part IV** _____

━━━━━━━━━━━━━━━━━━━━━━━━▶ **THE BOTTOM LINE**

Integration is not always the best way to grow. Bells and whistles sometimes contribute added value, but sometimes simply make a lot of noise.

Scenario #84
Moving Upstream

Despite the recent turndown in the business cycle, Allstar Aluminum, one of the leading producers of finished aluminum products, finds itself in an attractive cash position. As one of the shapers of company policy, you have decided that some upstream integration is in order and are planning to add an aluminum-mining operation in order to have a more reliable supply of the metal. This should also reduce potential costs due to market fluctuations in the price of aluminum. The overall weakness of the economy has put buyers in the driver's seat; and you don't want merely to integrate but also to get the best value for your investment dollar. Should you

▶ **A**

Take advantage of a newly discovered supply of bauxite in the western states and commence start-up operations?

or

▶ **B**

Purchase a well-managed aluminum-mining operation with a good track record?

or

▶ **C**

Buy a "weak sister" aluminum-mining operation and attempt to restore it to robust good health?

⟶

Solutions #84: **Moving Upstream**

A Take advantage of a newly discovered supply of bauxite in the western states and commence start-up operations?

▶ **–3 points** There are tremendous capital requirements necessary to start mining operations from scratch, to say nothing of the problems involved with recruiting reliable management and labor. This is the type of move that can fail completely, with disastrous consequences.

B Purchase a well-managed aluminum-mining operation with a good track record?

▶ **3 points** While this might minimize some problems because the firm is doing well, there is liable to be some resistance to change. Additionally, the initial capital requirements to take over a thriving organization figures to be substantial, because a successful acquisition would have to give away almost all of the perceived dollar gains to the seller.

C Buy a "weak sister" aluminum-mining operation and attempt to restore it to robust good health?

▶ **5 points** Although it may at first sight seem a case of "throwing good money after bad," there are several potentially highly favorable factors. The first is that it has what you need, namely an aluminum-mining operation. The second is that you can create an assured market for some of its products. Becoming part of Allstar's operations may well eliminate or reduce some of the reasons that the firm is doing poorly. Finally, companies are often undervalued in a recession. The only real threat to the success of this plan is a bad management team, and you may have to install one of your own.

Score _____   **Running Score for Part IV** _____

━━━━━━━━━━━━━━━━━━━━━━━━━━━━━━▶ **THE BOTTOM LINE**

Because assets are usually fairly priced, you are probably not paying too much by buying a poorly performing company, and the upside potential can be enormous. The most economical way to own swans is to buy ugly ducklings.

Scenario #85

Dog Meat

It's a dog-eat-dog world out there, and the dog food business is no exception. Just go into a supermarket and take a look; not only are there companies whose only business is the production of dog food, but titans of the food industry take their leftovers and try to peddle it to pooches. Nonetheless, you feel that you have what it takes to become a competitor in canine cuisine, and have persuaded a major meat-packer to forward integrate his operations by manufacturing dog food. The question is which sector of the market to attack, as there are several possibilities. Should you

▶ **A**

Take advantage of the meat-packer's savings on both manufacturing and distribution costs to market an inexpensive dog food?

or

▶ **B**

Persuade the meat-packer to let you have a few leftovers from the choice and prime cuts, and concentrate on the carriage trade?

or

▶ **C**

Scout around for the particular requirements of a popular breed, and try to sell specifically for oodles of poodles?

⟶

Solutions #85: **Dog Meat**

A Take advantage of the meat-packer's savings on both manufacturing and distribution costs to market an inexpensive dog food?

▶ **5 points**   Generally, if you can join the competitive low-cost leadership group in a market, you should do so. In particular, you are in an advantageous position here, as you not only can get meat by-products at a discount, but you can also obtain substantial savings on such other areas as packaging and distribution. Any other line of action throws away many of these advantages.

B Persuade the meat-packer to let you have a few leftovers from the choice and prime cuts, and concentrate on the carriage trade?

▶ **3 points**   This is a situation in which you can be guaranteed a market niche through product differentiation. Dogs are popular pets for the well-to-do, and the fact is that it's never a dog's life for any pooch owned by a fat cat. Additionally, your proximity to the meat-packing business will enable you to effect substantial savings. Here you are aiming at a rather small segment, which will limit your growth, but it will also substantially limit your risks.

C Scout around for the particular requirements of a popular breed, and try to sell specifically for oodles of poodles?

▶ **–1 point**   You would be shooting yourself in the foot if you tried this approach, as you would need to first find out if there is a need, and then if there is a market. There are many instances in which focusing on a particular market sector is an advisable strategy, but this is not one of them.

Score _____   **Running Score for Part IV** _____

━━━━━━━━━━━━━━━━━━━━━━━━━━▶ **THE BOTTOM LINE**

Integration often leads to savings in costs, and the most straightforward way to use these savings is to aim for low-cost leadership. Lowered costs are far more likely to lead to an increased market share if you're selling Fords than if you're selling Ferraris.

Scenario #86

Totally Compatible

Early in the computer game you realized that trouble was brewing in the future, as people with different computer systems ran into compatibility problems. While other companies were concentrating on building better and faster computers, you worked on developing integrators that could tie disparate systems together, so that Apples could talk to IBMs, and Compaqs could talk to Suns in peace and harmony. As a result, you've become one of the world's leaders in this exceptionally important area of computer technology. Your income statements are overflowing with black ink, and it's time to expand. There's nowhere to go horizontally, so you have decided to integrate vertically. Would you be best served by

▶ **A**

Buying a sick or dying company that manufactures personal computers and marketing them along with your integrators?

or

▶ **B**

Purchasing a semiconductor manufacturer so that you can save costs and design your own chips?

or

▶ **C**

Purchasing a sales and marketing firm so that you can take control of these functions in-house?

➡

Solutions #86: **Totally Compatible**

A Buying a sick or dying company that manufactures personal computers and marketing them along with your integrators?

▶ **–3 points** Who needs the aggravation? There is doubtless a reason that this company is going belly-up, and even though it would be cheap to purchase, you would probably dump a lot of money into it trying to make it competitive. Even more important, how will it add to the profitability of your main source of income, your integrators? Pass on this one.

B Purchasing a semiconductor manufacturer so that you can save costs and design your own chips?

▶ **5 points** There are obvious advantages here. By purchasing an upstream source of supply, you can control the reliability and supply of an important component of your business, to say nothing of the advantage that you will get having your integrator architects work hand in hand with the chip designers. They will benefit by having an assured market for some of their output. Another point is that this move is likely to raise mobility barriers for nonintegrated firms. The best deals are those which are good for both parties, and this is an obvious example.

C Purchasing a sales and marketing firm so that you can take control of these functions in-house?

▶ **I point** This is rather like trying to strengthen a football team by getting a better second-string punter. While the team will doubtless improve, at best it won't be by much. The rewards of this option are not large enough to justify the costs involved in getting away from your areas of expertise.

Score _____   **Running Score for Part IV** _____

━━━━━━━━━━━━━━━━━━━━━━━━━━━▶ **THE BOTTOM LINE**

Vertical integration is often most successful when the acquiring company can not only use the product of the acquired company but can contribute to its design and production. Rather than ask van Gogh to paint pictures to fit into frames, it is easier to design frames for his pictures.

Rock 'n' Roll

You came up with this truly novel concept, which absolutely revolutionized the rock music industry. You took four normal-looking guys; gave them haircuts; dressed them in slacks and sports coats; and placed them in front of an audience, playing guitars and pianos, and singing songs that had actual melodies and comprehensible lyrics. Far out, dude! As a result, the last five albums of your group, The Four Singers, have all gone platinum, their world tour is sold out for three years in the future, and kids the world over are starting to look like human beings again. Almost everywhere you look, people are hitting you with offers to set up performances. As the business manager, you are considering alternate possibilities for expansion, including backward and forward integration. Should you

▶ **A**

Purchase a clothes company that manufactures slacks and sports coats, and work out some sort of tie-in between them and your group?

or

▶ **B**

Look for a down-at-the-heels recording company, buy them out, and start putting out your albums under your own label?

or

▶ **C**

Purchase a music company that has the rights to some oldies-but-goodies and have your group rerecord them?

⟶

Solutions #87: **Rock 'n' Roll**

A Purchase a clothes company that manufactures slacks and sports coats, and work out some sort of tie-in between them and your group?

▶ **–I point**   Sing two choruses of "Call Me Irresponsible." It is certainly possible that the success of your group will cause an up-swing in the purchase of casual attire, but most of the clothes this company manufactures figures to be sold to people who were already buying this type of wearing apparel before The Four Singers came on the scene.

B Look for a down-at-the-heels recording company, buy them out, and start putting out your albums under your own label?

▶ **5 points**   Sing two choruses from "Who Could Ask for Anything More?" Here is the ideal synergy. You have the product they are lacking. You'll be purchasing a cheap asset, which will immediately benefit from recording your albums; you'll cut down your own costs and get a bigger share of the profits to boot.

C Purchase a music company that has the rights to some oldies-but-goodies and have your group rerecord them?

▶ **2 points**   Sing the refrain from "Chances Are." The chances are that this will work out nicely, but the way things are going your group could record the C-major scale and make a mint. This doesn't figure to produce the maximum value added.

Score _____   **Running Score for Part IV** _____

━━━━━━━━━━━━━━━━━━━━━━━━━━━▶ **THE BOTTOM LINE**

Integration should serve a purpose beyond that of simple acquisition. A synergistic whole is greater than the sum of its parts.

Scenario #88

Sawed Off

There's trouble downstream, both metaphorically and literally. A few years ago your profitable logging operation decided to purchase a sawmill at the end of the river down which you floated the logs, figuring that this would be a natural forward integration move. Unfortunately, the sawmill is not simply cutting the logs, it is reducing the profits of the parent corporation to sawdust, and this is creating a whole lot of problems for the entire operation. The logging operation has been persuaded to sell its logs below cost to the sawmill to make the income statements for the sawmill look even remotely respectable. As CEO of the entire corporation, you've got to reduce your losses. Should you

▶ **A**

Get rid of the sawmill altogether, as it has turned out to be not an asset but a liability?

   or

▶ **B**

Stick with the status quo; after all, when you bought the sawmill, you didn't think you were buying a lemon?

   or

▶ **C**

Assist the sawmill through the parent entity, but stop this nonsense about selling logs to the sawmill below cost?

━━▶

Solutions #88: **Sawed Off**

A Get rid of the sawmill altogether, as it has turned out to be not an asset but a liability?

▶ **5 points**   One of the hardest things to do is to acknowledge that you have made a mistake. This is one of those decisions that look easy on paper—both the paper of this book and the paper you as CEO will read when you look at the numbers—but it can often be a difficult decision to make in the real world. As CEO, you simply have to stop the bleeding. The acquisition is not performing as planned and shows no promise of doing so.

B Stick with the status quo; after all, when you bought the sawmill, you didn't think you were buying a lemon?

▶ **0 points**   New information has entered the picture, and sticking with the status quo fails to recognize the value of that information. Unfortunately, no warning buzzers sound to indicate that bad things are beginning to happen, and it is the reaction to new information that makes the difference in the long run between winning and losing decisions.

C Assist the sawmill through the parent entity, but stop this nonsense about selling logs to the sawmill below cost?

▶ **3 points**   If you decide to try to save the sawmill, this is the best way. By forcing the logging operations to bear some of the loss, you are shouldering them with an unnecessary burden and reducing the incentive for them to do well. Simply changing the accounting allocation would probably add visibility to the problem, shed light on the relative responsibilities, and could suggest solutions. Even though this sawmill is not competitive despite the fact that it has an assured market, there are sawmills that do operate profitably. The parent entity should probably consider bringing in a consultant.

Score _____   **Running Score for Part IV** _____

━━━━━━━━━━━━━━━━━━━━━━━━━━▶ **THE BOTTOM LINE**

When results don't go according to plan, the plan must be reevaluated. To err is human, to fail to admit it can be costly.

10

Major Capacity Expansion

THE ISSUES

Because of its important consequences, both to the industry and the firm, there is no more formidable decision than one involving major capacity expansion. It is imperative, therefore, that any firm contemplating capacity expansion evaluate its position (portfolio of commitments) resulting from each of its contemplated actions.

The larger the ratio of added capacity to current capacity, the more significant is the firm's decision. If a large firm decides to build one more factory, the incremental capacity may represent only a small percentage, and the effect of the decision may be relatively minor. For a firm consisting of one factory to build another, however, is an altogether different situation. Success can change the nature of the firm, setting it on a course that may eventually lift it into a higher league. Failure may be catastrophic, leading to the firm's demise.

Decision Theory, Game Theory

Major capacity expansion decisions are complex problems, which utilize the disciplines of both decision theory and game theory. The dominant variables in decision theory are the various states of the environment, such as possible levels of demand, changes in regulations, etc., for which the firm needs to make forecasts and estimate probabilities. Game theory, on the other hand, deals with more difficult problems, where the dominant variables may be the sometimes malevolent actions of competitors.

A firm's competitors may act malevolently when they are using a short-term planning horizon, and their interests are in opposition to those of the firm. In such circumstances, the firm should consider defending itself using the minimax criterion for its decisions. To utilize this criterion, the firm would examine the worst possible outcome from each possible action and then choose the action for which the worst possible outcome is as good as it can be.

In most situations, however, competitors have important common interests, such as increasing total industry demand or avoiding catastrophic price cutting and retaliation. So it is not appropriate to focus completely on the worst possible outcomes. Decision making in such circumstances is far more complex.

Not only must the firm contemplating major capacity expansion consider its own possible actions and their concomitant payoffs, but it must realize that payoffs also depend to an important degree upon actions that might be taken by competitors, as well as upon the probabilities of future states of demand. The firm must therefore make forecasts of the future extent and timing of demand. It must also analyze the motivations of its competitors, make forecasts from their points of view, and even try to influence the actions of its competitors. Such influence may take several forms. A firm with a respected position in the industry may issue credible advance market signals to deter competitors, or it may take decisive preemptive actions.

Preemptive Actions

Preemptive actions are those which, when taken, effectively prevent competitors from taking similar action. Preemptive actions not only deter present competitors from taking action, they also have the potential to raise entry barriers, thereby discouraging other companies from entering the industry. Whether or not a given action will have a preemptive effect depends on both the firm taking the action and its competitors. Preemptive actions are highly aggressive moves; a move intended as preemptive by a small firm is unlikely to be so.

Similarly, because the reaction to aggression is not always completely rational, a move intended as preemptive may not have the desired effect. One of the difficulties in attempting to forecast reactions by competitors to capacity expansion is that these reactions are not always made from purely economic considerations. Some competitors may place a premium on prestige, some may not back down because it is deemed undesirable to show weakness, and still others may have a longer time horizon, requiring them to make different decisions than firms considering only short-term results.

Risks

Major capacity expansion decisions are fraught with risk. Overcapacity greatly intensifies competition and severely reduces profit margins, as companies try to utilize their excess capacity. While undercapacity is short-lived because firms will quickly expand, or because new entrants will be attracted, overcapacity must wait for demand to increase, a condition which is not always quickly forthcoming.

Some industries are prone to problems stemming from overcapacity. Prominent among these are industries producing commoditylike products, essentially interchangeable, with little or no differentiation. In such industries, demand for the products is often cyclical, and occasional overly optimistic predictions of future demand leads to simultaneous long-term capacity expansion by many of the companies in the industry. Additionally, the fact that the products themselves are not differentiated leads potential buyers to base their purchasing decisions primarily on cost. Attempts to reduce cost often require capacity expansion in order to achieve greater economies of scale. However, because many of the firms in the industry will simultaneously attempt to achieve those economies of scale, overcapacity often results.

It is also important to consider the state of the industry in making the decision to expand. Obviously, the analysis of future demand is predicated on realizing whether the industry is in the growth, maturity, or declining phase of industry evolution. In general, a reasonable principle to follow is that the more aggressive the decision, the less its chances for success in the latter phases of industry evolution.

Scenario #89
Black Monday

Remember Black Monday? That incredible Monday morning in Oc-
tober 1987, when the Dow Jones Industrial Average plunged more
than 500 points? You not only remember it, you were one of the
few portfolio managers to predict it. More importantly, you got your
investors out before the crash. Were they grateful? Back in 1987,
they were singing your praises, but in the portfolio management
game, it's "what have you done for me lately?" Lately, the market
has been booming, and you've been only partially invested. Your super-
visors have been breathing down your neck. You are virtually alone
again in the belief that disaster is imminent. Nonetheless, your job
is on the line. Are you more likely to survive by

▶ **A**

Increasing the equity portion of your portfolio, even though by
going along with the herd you are going against your better
judgment?

   or

▶ **B**

Hedging your bet by standing pat, doing worse than the crowd
if the market goes up but doing better if it goes down?

   or

▶ **C**

Backing your judgment to the hilt by selling the equity portion
of your portfolio and waiting for the expected replay of Black
Monday?

                                                    ⟶

Solutions #89: **Black Monday**

A Increasing the equity portion of your portfolio, even though by going along with the herd you are going against your better judgment?

▶ **5 points**   The problem you face is similar to the one faced by an industrial manager deciding whether to expand capacity in the face of increasing capacity and demand. The manager takes no blame by being wrong WITH the crowd, but his position is in jeopardy if he is wrong ALONE. You, personally, have more to lose by staying out of an up market than by getting into a down market in which everyone gets clobbered. You were a hero back in 1987, it isn't necessary to be one again.

B Hedging your bet by standing pat, doing worse than the crowd if the market goes up but doing better if it goes down?

▶ **I point**   The underlying principle is still the same. If you are going to make the wrong move, it's best to be sure that you have plenty of company. This herd instinct explains why managers can plunge an industry into overcapacity by exhibiting an asymmetrical aversion to risk.

C Backing your judgment to the hilt by selling the equity portion of your portfolio and waiting for the expected replay of Black Monday?

▶ **−2 points**   Disaster city. You have to be incredibly sure of yourself to make a move like this, as it is the riskiest position you could possibly take. If you are wrong, and the market continues up, you're history. The stock market is a leading indicator, and those who continually manage to lead a leading indicator are few and far between.

Score _____   **Running Score for Part IV** _____

━━━━━━━━━━━━━━━━━━━━━━━━━━━━━▶ **THE BOTTOM LINE**

Managers often stand to lose more by being the last to expand capacity in a strong market than they do by having overexpanded with the crowd in a weak one. A loser is more noticeable in a gathering of winners than in a convention of losers.

Scenario #90

Cash Crop

The giant agricultural chemicals firm of which you have been an important part for more than twenty years finds itself in the delightful position of having an unwieldy amount of cash. You are in the process of figuring out what to do with it. There are reliable rumors that your only major competitor is going to phase out some of its plants over the next ten years or so, and go in for an extensive R & D program on the application of genetic engineering to agriculture. What to do with all that cash? Should you

▶ **A**

Invest in additional capacity, planning on grabbing an increased market share if and when your chief competitor pulls out?

   or

▶ **B**

Take the money, get a competitive short-term rate in the market, and await developments?

   or

▶ **C**

Start an R & D program yourself, figuring that you had better not be left behind if genetic engineering is the coming thing?

⟶

Solutions #90: **Cash Crop**

A Invest in additional capacity, planning on grabbing an increased market share if and when your chief competitor pulls out?

▶ **–3 points**   Expanding capacity is an offensive move that is normally taken in an industry undergoing rapid growth. The mere fact that you have a lot of cash indicates that the industry and your position in it are on the defensive. This is *not* a time when the best defense is a good offense.

B Take the money, get a competitive short-term rate in the market, and await developments?

▶ **2 points**   This would certainly not be the worst move ever made. As someone once observed, impetuosity is a virtue only when delay is dangerous. You can earn a competitive rate while waiting to see which way the chips will fall. Being a cash cow may make you an attractive takeover candidate as well.

C Start an R & D program yourself, figuring that you had better not be left behind if genetic engineering is the coming thing?

▶ **5 points**   If your major competitor is going to do this, you want to make sure that you are not left at the starting gate. Leaders in mature industries often take an abnormal amount of time to realize that the winds of change are blowing. If genetic engineering is the wave of the future, you could easily find yourself going from a leading position in a mature industry to the last relic of a moribund one.

Score _____   **Running Score for Part IV** _____

━━━━━━━━━━━━━━━━━━━━━━━━━━━━▶ **THE BOTTOM LINE**

Research programs are often a form of insurance; if unsuccessful, you are out the cost of the premium, if successful, you have hedged against a possible disaster. An ounce of foresight is worth a pound of hindsight.

Scenario #91

Onward and Upward

Your helicopter firm, Whirlybirds, Inc., has managed to establish a comfortable niche for itself producing medium-sized helicopters, which it has sold to a variety of small businesses. Both the industry and the firm are flying high, and the next few years will undoubtedly see a lot more choppers in the air. Whirlybirds' management is set on expansion, but the direction of that expansion is not at all clear. It is up to you to come up with an appropriate plan that will lead Whirlybirds onward and upward. Should you

▶ **A**

Continue along the present course of manufacturing medium-sized helicopters but increase your capacity?

or

▶ **B**

Succumb to the lure of a highly profitable government contract, which would require you to manufacture a heavier-duty helicopter and equip it for military use?

or

▶ **C**

Expand your product line by manufacturing a smaller, cheaper helicopter, or maybe a larger luxury model?

$$\Longrightarrow$$

Solutions #91: **Onward and Upward**

A Continue along the present course of manufacturing medium-sized helicopters, but increase your capacity?

▶ **5 points**   If the industry as a whole is doing well, and your firm has located a profitable niche in that industry, why would you want to change a winning strategy? This is clearly a time to dance with the girl you brought to the party.

B Succumb to the lure of a highly profitable government contract, which would require you to manufacture a heavier-duty helicopter and equip it for military use?

▶ **2 points**   On the upside, government contracting can be a lucrative gravy train, and you could end up rolling in money. On the other hand, switching to a different model, perhaps requiring a complete change in the manufacturing structure, could backfire if you don't meet the specifications of the contract, or if the government doesn't renew it. Another negative feature is that there is nothing a government bureaucracy loves better than to create and shuffle papers, and the drastic changes in quantity and methods of documentation could upset the entire company.

C Expand your product line by manufacturing a smaller, cheaper helicopter, or maybe a larger luxury model?

▶ **−1 point**   This is one of the classic traps in the management game. Having succeeded in one area, the formerly keen vision of the company leadership suddenly becomes clouded with visions of sugarplums. Think of other firms with established niches. Is Mercedes producing cheap subcompacts? Is McDonald's selling filet mignon?

Score _____   **Running Score for Part IV** _____

━━━━━━━━━━━━━━━━━━━━━━━━━━━━━▶ **THE BOTTOM LINE**

Expansion need not always go hand in hand with diversification. You can stick to your niche and still find new worlds to conquer if you want to expand.

Scenario #92

Laugh Track

It's been a good year for sitcoms. The Nielsen ratings have sitcoms occupying five of the top ten slots, and advertisers are lining up to get a piece of next year's action. As program director for the current number one network in the popularity poll, you realize that sitcoms are hot, while westerns and cop shows are not. Nonetheless, you are wondering about the advisability of adding more sitcoms to your already chock-full lineup, while simultaneously casting a sideways glance at the other major networks. What are they going to do? If everybody goes sitcom happy, there may not be enough laughs to go around. You'd better make the right decision, or you'll be an ex-program director for the number two or three network. Should you

▶ **A**

   Assume that the airwaves will be saturated with sitcoms and line up something else?

   or

▶ **B**

   Schedule as many sitcoms as your writers can produce and get the message out to the advertisers as soon as possible?

   or

▶ **C**

   Announce that you are considering scheduling extra sitcoms and see how the other major networks react?

⟶

Solutions #92: **Laugh Track**

A Assume that the airwaves will be saturated with sitcoms and line up something else?

▶ **-2 points**   When all the other industry managers are expanding capacity in the face of increasing demand, you've got to have a mammoth ego to buck the trend. This being Hollywood, perhaps you do, but why be a hero when you don't have to? Even if you are wrong, the others will also be wrong, and maybe you can still hang on to your number one rating.

B Schedule as many sitcoms as your writers can produce and get the message out to the advertisers as soon as possible?

▶ **5 points**   It's war here, and you'd better launch a preemptive strike in order to capture as many objectives (advertisers' dollars) as possible. The advertisers know what they want, sitcoms, and if you don't get there to tickle their collective funny bones, the other major networks are going to have the last laugh.

C Announce that you are considering scheduling extra sitcoms and see how the other major networks react?

▶ **1 point**   Here's how the other major networks will react. They will schedule sitcoms. The advertisers, who are lining up to back sitcoms, are not going to be interested in what you say you might do but what others will do.

Score _____   **Running Score for Part IV** _____

———————————————————————————▶ **THE BOTTOM LINE**

In a race to expand capacity, there is a big premium placed on being one of the first. If you hit first, your opponent may be unwilling or unable to hit back.

Scenario #93

Noise Makers

The public calls them jackhammers, but to you they'll always be pneumatic drills. A jackhammer by any other name can still make enough sound to wake the dead. More importantly, they generate enough profit to keep your business, which is manufacturing and distributing these devices, in the black. It's a good, steady business, but unless there's a sudden building boom on the moon or earth-quakes devastate Russia, and you are called in to do the rebuilding job, you don't see any dramatic upswing in demand. Nonetheless, the engineers at your plant have not been asleep (how could they, with all that noise), and they have developed a way to generate economies of scale if you expand. This presents a problem. Should you

▶ **A**

Generate those economies of scale and expand, figuring that it will enable you to seize low-cost leadership of the industry?

or

▶ **B**

Announce that you are contemplating expansion and see how the other jackhammer producers react?

or

▶ **C**

Stand pat, figuring that in a constant demand market you don't want to run the risk of overcapacity?

⟶

Solutions #93: **Noise Makers**

A Generate those economies of scale and expand, figuring that it will enable you to seize low-cost leadership of the industry?

▶ **5 points**   Go for it. Being the low-cost leader in an industry gives a powerful competitive advantage. Even if you cause slight overcapacity, your lower cost will allow profitable operations at a lower price. The increased capacity will also greatly discourage your competitors from expanding and achieving the same economies of scale.

B Announce that you are contemplating expansion and see how the other jackhammer producers react?

▶ **–2 points**   Here's how the other jackhammer producers will react. Their spokespersons will make noncommittal remarks, while they turn up the sound of the jackhammers at their factories to keep *their* engineers up late at night. They will achieve economies of scale, and the added capacity will keep you from following.

C Stand pat, figuring that in a constant demand market you don't want to run the risk of overcapacity?

▶ **0 points**   Admittedly, you now have a trump card that you can play when conditions improve. In general, though, you don't want to do what bridge players describe as "going to sleep with an ace"; failing to play a winning card at a critical time, and later losing it because you failed to play it.

Score _____   **Running Score for Part IV** _____

━━━━━━━━━━━━━━━━━━━━━━━━━━━▶ **THE BOTTOM LINE**

It is worth taking risks to achieve economies of scale, because this places you in position to seize low-cost leadership. The bigger the reward, the bigger the risk you should be willing to take.

Scenario #94

Steel Yourself

It has taken several decades, but finally America has managed to iron out some of the major problems concerning its steel industry. Contributing to this happy state of affairs are an increasing reliance on robotics, the weakness of the dollar vis-à-vis the yen, and the fact that it is cheaper to mine iron and mill steel in the United States than to ship iron to and from Japan. As a result your company, which is the leading steel producer and industry statesperson in the United States, is once again on top. You and the other major steel producers are facing increasing demand, and everyone is looking to expand capacity. This might not work out too well, as overcapacity would be looming on the horizon. Should you

▶ **A**

Preemptively expand your capacity, figuring that because you are the largest producer you will end up with the lion's share of the market?

or

▶ **B**

Announce that you are planning to expand and then expand, figuring that the other producers will realize the dangers of overcapacity?

or

▶ **C**

Stay where you are because when the other producers expand, your added capacity would precipitate industrywide disaster?

⟶

Solutions #94: **Steel Yourself**

A Preemptively expand your capacity, figuring that because you are the largest producer you will end up with the lion's share of the market?

▶ **I point**   The good news is that you are likely to end up with a profit. The bad news is that this approach does not maximize your profit, it makes your profit less likely. If everyone expands, over-capacity is a distinct possibility, and simply expanding does not send a timely market signal that might allay this threat.

B Announce that you are planning to expand and then expand, figuring that the other producers will realize the dangers of overcapacity?

▶ **5 points**   Who said that virtue is its own reward? All those years as the industry statesperson, coupled with your leading position, is going to pay *big* dividends in the oligopoly that is the steel industry. Announce your plans for expansion while delivering a states-personlike address, in which you caution against the dangers of un-restricted greed. Although actions may speak louder than words, in this instance the appropriate words backed up by actions have greater preemptive value than the actions alone.

C Stay where you are because when the other producers expand, your added capacity would precipitate industrywide disaster?

▶ **−2 points**   This is not merely turning the other cheek, it is courting disaster. If the pie is going to get larger, there is no reason for Snow White to be content with her lot while the Seven Dwarfs all stuff themselves. The added capacity of the other producers fig-ures to lower the price of steel. *They*, not you, will have generated extra volume to offset this.

Score _____   **Running Score for Part IV** _____

━━━━━━━━━━━━━━━━━━━━━━━━━━━▶ **THE BOTTOM LINE**

Preemptive announcements, followed by action, can minimize the threat of overcapacity. In order to have your cake and eat it, too, it is sometimes necessary to say, "This is MY cake!"

11

Entering an Industry

THE ISSUES

Of all the major decisions that it is possible for a firm to make, the decision to enter an industry is perhaps the most critical. All the major questions on which this book has focused bear upon this question, so it is fitting to conclude with an examination of this decision.

The Firm's Strategy

A firm contemplating entry into a different industry must realize there is a distinct possibility that such entry may change the nature of the firm by involving it with a different fundamental strategy. A firm must concentrate on either a broad or narrow market focus, and either strive for low-cost leadership or product differentiation within this sector. The successful firm will have achieved a certain amount of expertise within the confines of its general strategic approach and will have built a structure and process to implement that strategy. For example, a structure and process that rationalizes a profitable product differentiation strategy within a narrow market focus in a particular industry may well be transferable into a similar strategy pursued in the entered industry.

Contrariwise, there is no reason to think that a successful narrow market, product differentiator will be well equipped to carry out a broad market, low-cost strategy in the entered industry. Indeed, entry into an industry requiring a different strategic approach on the part of the entering firm typically requires a costly, time-consuming, and risky change in company structure and process, and therefore should be viewed with a skeptical eye.

Acquisition versus Development

An existing company wanting to enter a new industry can do so either by acquiring a firm already in the industry, or by developing a new product, its necessary manufacturing process, and the requisite organizational structure. Entry through development will add capacity to the industry, which can trigger price cutting and thereby increase the risk of retaliation by existing firms. Target industries for entry with new capacity should be those in which retaliation is least likely to occur and include those where demand will soon exceed the present capacity (such as industries in the growth phase). Target industries may be those in which the incumbent firms are inefficient, are not strong competitors, are small, or would have a high cost of retaliation.

When entering an industry by acquisition, the firm is buying an asset (the acquired company), whose price is determined fairly by the market. If the acquiring firm has a unique ability to improve the operations of the firm it acquires, or if the acquisition uniquely helps the purchaser's existing business, then the market price may be an advantageous one for the buyer. Because that knowledge is widely shared, the firm being acquired generally extracts a generous premium to induce its shareholders to sell to the acquiring firm.

All the important questions examined earlier bear upon the question of entry into a new industry. Consider, for instance, the problem of isolating the dominant variables. These may not necessarily be the same ones that are dominant for the firm in its present state. An analysis of the new variables will help determine whether the acquiring firm possesses a unique ability to improve the operations of the existing firm, or whether the acquired firm can help the purchaser's existing business.

An investment in a new industry can be viewed either as a probable source of above average returns or as a risk-reduction vehicle, as when a conglomerate consisting of many unrelated companies decides to acquire yet another unrelated company. Alternatively, the industry may be entered as an integration move, in which case all the questions pertaining to the advisability of integration must be carefully examined. Sometimes a firm may be motivated to buy a cash cow in a declining industry in order to supply funds for an expanding business.

Knowing the Industry and the Firm

Obviously, it is important to assess the evolutionary state of the industry being entered. Entry into a new or growing industry poses different risks than entry into a mature industry, in which the competition is liable to be fierce. Entering an industry that appears to be in the decline phase should present small risk, typically in the form of a very high probability of stable returns. The company considering entry into a new industry must know itself well, perhaps better than a company that is not contemplating such a move. In addition to the danger that the acquiring firm may be unprepared to cope with an expanded scale of operations, acquisitions typically create added complexity when the systems are merged. Results are similar in thermodynamics, where the entropy, a measure of disorder, of a combined system is greater than the sum of the entropies of the separate systems. Problems may be introduced relating to both the operating processes and the responsibility and authority structures of the acquiring and acquired companies.

A temporary euphoria, based on both fiscal and psychological factors, may result in an unwise entry into an industry. Indeed, the successful manager is often an optimist, and nowhere is this more strongly evidenced than in the entry phase. It is easy to see nothing but blue skies ahead while looking at the recent performance of the firm, the state of the industry to be entered, the nature of the projected competition, and in the economy as a whole. During this period, it is important to read all the indicators and analyze conflicting signals. For instance, seeing the potential competition in disarray may induce the overly optimistic to envision easy pickings, without paying sufficient. attention to the possibility that weakened competition may be the consequence of an unfavorable industry environment. To guard against this trap, the decision not to enter must always be regarded as a serious alternative.

Scenario #95

Safe Venture

As manager of the Bee Safe Company, whose motto, needless to say, is "Better Bee Safe than be sorry," you have been doing quite nicely manufacturing high-quality, precision-crafted safes. However, you have been infuriated by the fact that you manufacture 600 pounds of high-quality safe, and reap the same profit as the manufacturer who supplies you with the 5 pounds of electronic lock that is installed in the door of your safe. The obvious solution is to break into the lock business, and fortunately you have a reasonable supply of capital to finance such an investment. The critical decision is how great a commitment you should make. Is it better to

▶ **A**

Play it safe and stick to what you know best, putting your excess cash in the bank?

or

▶ **B**

Purchase a small lock manufacturer and equip some of your safes with the lock to see whether this is a workable idea?

or

▶ **C**

Find a major manufacturer who can supply all your needs and purchase it, lock, stock, and barrel?

⟶

Solutions #95: **Safe Venture**

A Play it safe and stick to what you know best, putting your excess cash in the bank?

▶ **2 points**   No one would be surprised by a conservative move from a manufacturer of safes, and there is certainly nothing wrong with making a sensible decision. However, most companies try to grow, and sticking your money in a bank is not the way to do it. Sometimes, if you don't make dust, you eat dust.

B Purchase a small lock manufacturer and equip some of your safes with the lock to see whether this is a workable idea?

▶ **5 points**   A sequenced entry into a new business is the ideal way to enter a new business. Theoretically, this is a natural merger, which will increase your profits, but theory and practice are often quite different. If this works, you will be in an excellent position to lock up added profits; if it fails, the minimum amount of damage will have been done. An alternative would be some form of quasi integration, in which you make an alliance with a lock manufacturer.

C Find a major manufacturer who can supply all your needs and purchase it, lock, stock, and barrel?

▶ **–I point**   On the surface, it seems like a good idea, but it could turn out badly. When entering a new business, there are always risks of which the buyer is unaware, and sequenced entry enables the entrant to be in a better position to judge the risks, rewards, and probability of success than an irreversible all-out plunge. Flexible decisions are rarely heavily penalized.

Score _____   **Running Score for Part IV** _____

━━━━━━━━━━━━━━━━━━━━━━━━▶ **THE BOTTOM LINE**

A sequenced entry into a new business allows for a more accurate estimation of risks and rewards without assuming unnecessary risks. Frequently, when you go for broke, you go broke.

Scenario #96

Iron Horse

The CEO of the conglomerate for which you work must have played too much Monopoly without a helmet when he was a child; suddenly, he has exhibited a mania for acquiring a railroad and getting into interstate transportation. Most of your fiscal future is tied up in stock options, and you foresee the company's stock taking a major hit if this deal goes through. You'd like to write a detailed plan outlining the major flaws with this idea, but there is only time for a short but trenchant memo in which you point out the chief liability involved in owning a railroad, which is

▶ **A**

The decline in the status of the railroads as a force in shipping; they are losing ground to trucking and airlines.

   or

▶ **B**

The vulnerability of the system to a strike by any one of several key groups affiliated with the railroad industry.

   or

▶ **C**

The difficulty of finding another buyer in case the investment proves the lemon you think it will be.

⟶

Solutions #96: **Iron Horse**

A   The decline in the status of the railroads as a force in shipping; they are losing ground to trucking and airlines.

▶ **1 point**   It is certainly true that, as Arlo Guthrie said of the City of New Orleans, "this train's got the disappearing railroad blues." Nonetheless, a railroad train has tremendous carrying capacity to compensate for its lack of speed, and there will doubtless be a need for them in the foreseeable future, even though they will probably lose ground to the other shipping industries.

B   The vulnerability of the system to a strike by any one of several key groups affiliated with the railroad industry.

▶ **–1 point**   Strikes are not that much of a danger in an industry that is undergoing decline. Jobs will be disappearing in the industry, and strikers will worry that, if they walk off the job, the job may disappear entirely. This isn't to say that strikes can't happen (after all, they certainly did during the Depression), but potential strikes are not a major source of worry for the potential investor.

C   The difficulty of finding another buyer in case the investment proves the lemon you think it will be.

▶ **5 points**   A declining industry is like musical chairs; when the music stops, there are a lot more people (sellers) looking to sit down than there are chairs (buyers). Unless the purchase can be made on unbelievably favorable financial terms, the height of the exit barriers in the railroad industry is a major concern.

Score _____   **Running Score for Part IV** _____

━━━━━━━━━━━━━━━━━━━━━▶ **THE BOTTOM LINE**

The decision to enter an industry should incorporate as a factor the height of the exit barriers. If you can see that you have trouble getting out, you may think twice about getting in.

Scenario #97

Nailed Down

In business, it's always important to get down to brass tacks. It's especially important in your business, because that's your business—brass tacks, as well as tacks and nails of every shape and variety. Business is good, the construction and related industries are booming, and you want your company to continue along its present course by expanding into the manufacture and distribution of screws, nuts, and bolts. Some of the other executives are dubious, pointing out that building and construction are cyclical industries dealing in basically interchangeable products, and that you can continue to nail down good profits by sticking with what you do best. It comes down to whether you can make above average returns. Should you

▶ **A**

Take the advice of your other executives and concentrate on backing what seems to be a sure winner, your current business?

or

▶ **B**

Find a nut, bolt, and screw manufacturer that can be purchased for a fair price and do so?

or

▶ **C**

Raise enough capital to become a new entrant and start a new business to manufacture nuts, bolts, and screws?

⟶

Solutions #97: **Nailed Down**

A Take the advice of your other executives and concentrate on backing what seems to be a sure winner, your current business?

▶ **3 points**   If your firm is conservative, and the penalty for failure is stronger than the reward for success, this might well be the best move. Sticking with a proven winner is rarely a bad strategy, especially in a climate in which the proven winner appears likely to continue doing so.

B Find a nut, bolt, and screw manufacturer that can be purchased for a fair price and do so?

▶ **5 points**   Business concerns, like living organisms, should be continually aware of the possibility for growth, otherwise they tend to stagnate. This is a good time to enter this particular industry by buying a going concern rather than increasing industry capacity for a mature, commoditylike product. In addition to the basic health of the industry, the business meshes nicely with yours.

C Raise enough capital to become a new entrant and start a new business to manufacture nuts, bolts, and screws?

▶ **1 point**   Although you will be making a fundamentally sound move, there are two reasons why this is not the best way to enter. First, you are manufacturing a commoditylike product, and this increases the threat of capacity-inspired retaliation. Additionally, the lead time required to build your own plant might bring it on-line towards the top of the business cycle.

Score _____   **Running Score for Part IV** _____

━━━━━━━━━━━━━━━━━━━━━━━━━▶ **THE BOTTOM LINE**

Capacity expansion of commoditylike goods is very likely to promote costly retaliation. When conditions are such that the lemming population rises dramatically one year, it almost invariably results in a suicidal dash for the sea.

Scenario #98

Wall Street

You've put in your time to get to the point where you have a chance to show your stuff. You've got all the essential prerequisites: an MBA from Harvard, a tour of duty with one of the big-time Wall Street brokerages, a power tie, and an intimate knowledge of how to conduct yourself at power lunches. While you don't necessarily agree with those in the industry who say that greed is good, as a newly hired member of the M & A team (that's mergers and acquisitions, for those of you not up on the lingo) of a major investment banking house you are greedy enough to want above average returns and feel you are good enough to get them. You've just bagged your first big client, a successfully managed oil firm loaded with cash, which is anxious to acquire and manage a business with good future profit growth potential. After surveying the landscape, you've narrowed the field to three companies. Should you recommend that it acquire

▶ **A**

An ocean thermal energy conversion (OTEC) company that could be a leader in a promising but untried technology?

   or

▶ **B**

An efficient, well-managed oil company with proven reserves, predictable output, good marketing contacts, and stable earnings?

   or

▶ **C**

A poorly managed natural gas company that holds a large number of leases on fields with unproven reserves?

⟶

Solutions #98: **Wall Street**

A An ocean thermal energy conversion (OTEC) company that could be a leader in a promising but untried technology?

▶ **0 points**   You've picked a chancy way to try to make above average returns. Most assets are fairly priced, and the price of this company reflects the fact that the technology is untried and unproven. If the technology succeeds, you will certainly show above average returns (by a lot); if it fails, you will show below average returns (also by a lot). Basically, you've selected a fancy, high-tech way to roll the dice.

B An efficient, well-managed oil company with proven reserves, predictable output, good marketing contacts, and stable earnings?

▶ **–1 point**   This company is already efficient and well managed, and there is no indication that the assets will be worth more after the acquisition. What you have here is an excellent candidate for average market return on your investment.

C A poorly managed natural gas company that holds a large number of leases on fields with unproven reserves?

▶ **5 points**   Companies with high turnaround potential are excellent candidates for above average returns on investment. The gas company is poorly managed, so you should be able to better utilize its assets, and there is uncertainty about the value of its leases, which adds to the investment potential by greatly depressing the market price. The natural gas and oil businesses are closely related, and your client is successful and well managed and therefore stands a fine chance of turning this turkey around.

Score _____   **Running Score for Part IV** _____

━━━━━━━━━━━━━━━━━━━━━━━━━━▶ **THE BOTTOM LINE**

When buying a poorly performing company, be sure you have a plan to make its assets worth more in *your* hands than in theirs. Manhattan Island was worth only $24 in the hands of the original owners.

Scenario #99

Media Merger

You are an up-and-coming executive of a major film manufacturer that currently finds itself with a fistful of dollars and is trying to decide whether or not it is likely to obtain above average returns by getting into the manufacture of floppy disks. The economy is doing well, and there are only a few relatively large firms manufacturing floppy disks, all of whom have healthy balance sheets. Because cameras use film and computers use floppy disks, it seems unlikely that you will be cutting your own throat by manufacturing floppy disks. Rather, the move should help expand your customer base for both products. The CEO has asked for your analysis; a promotion could be riding on it. Should you advise the firm to

▶ **A**

Enter the floppy disk manufacturing business by building a state-of-the-art complex to do this?

    or

▶ **B**

Buy out one of the current floppy disk manufacturers?

    or

▶ **C**

Abandon the idea of entering floppy disk manufacturing altogether and do something else with the excess cash?

$\longrightarrow$

Solutions #99: **Media Merger**

A Enter the floppy disk manufacturing business by building a state-of-the-art complex to do this?

▶ **–2 points**   No promotion for you and possibly no job as well. With only a few major firms in the business, the pressure to retaliate when you enter, perhaps even against your film business, will be fierce, as your added capacity figures to reduce everyone's profit margins. It also seems unlikely that you can improve your existing situation in the film industry by manufacturing floppy disks.

B Buy out one of the current floppy disk manufacturers?

▶ **0 points**   It's a bad time to be a buyer, because the economy is doing well and the major firms are profitable. Buyers always do better when either the economy is bad, or a potential seller is in trouble. Although you might improve your buying price by getting the sellers to compete, there is basically no reason to assume that you can obtain above average profits. It is true that buying into an existing firm would give you entry into the industry without increasing capacity and risking retaliation, but it is preferable to buy when either the price is low or one of the businesses involved in the transaction can help the other.

C Abandon the idea of entering floppy disk manufacturing altogether and do something else with the excess cash?

▶ **5 points**   Considering that if you want to enter internally you have to spend a lot of money and will provoke retaliation, if you want to acquire no one will sell to you at a good price, and there are no potential benefits to your existing business, what other choice is there?

Score _____   **Running Score for Part IV** _____

━━━━━━━━━━━━━━━━━━━━━━━━━━━▶ **THE BOTTOM LINE**

Retaliation is likely to be fiercest when there are a few major competitors than when there are a lot of little ones. It is much more dangerous to go swimming where there are a few sharks than where there are a lot of guppies.

Scenario #100

Star Struck

Is there life in outer space? Did a comet slam into earth 65 million years ago and kick up enough dust to block the sunlight and eventually kill the dinosaurs? These are fascinating questions, but even more fascinating to you is this one: Can all this interest in what's happening in the universe, which seems to be sustainable rather than simply faddish, be converted into above average returns on investment for your company? Your company is a major manufacturer of cameras and photographic equipment. While others are scanning the skies for comets and extraterrestrials, you are scanning the profit-and-loss statements of the companies that manufacture telescopes. You like what you see; even though not every company is doing well, the industry is undergoing meteoric growth. Would you recommend that the company

▶ **A**

Acquire a firm that is already manufacturing telescopes and try to dovetail it with your operation?

or

▶ **B**

Stay out of the telescope business entirely, remembering the immortal words falsely attributed to Sir Isaac Newton, "What goes up, must come down"?

or

▶ **C**

Get into the telescope business through the internal entry route and start from scratch to construct a new business entity?

➡

Solutions #100: **Star Struck**

A Acquire a firm that is already manufacturing telescopes and try to dovetail it with your operation?

▶ **3 points**   It would seem that there is every reason to enter the telescope industry, which is growing nicely and, additionally, figures to mesh well with your current operations. Both telescopes and cameras use lenses, and cameras are often coupled with telescopes to take pictures. The only flies in the ointment are that, by acquiring an existing operation, you will not achieve a perfect fit with your own operation, and you will probably have to pay a good price since the industry is very robust.

B Stay out of the telescope business entirely, remembering the immortal words falsely attributed to Sir Isaac Newton, "What goes up, must come down"?

▶ **–2 points**   Newton was a great scientist, but there is no record of his being a successful business manager. There is no better time to get into an industry than when it is growing, and no better industry to get into than one that fits with yours.

C Get into the telescope business through the internal entry route and start from scratch to construct a new business entity?

▶ **5 points**   All things considered, this is your best option. The time is right, the industry is right, and the advantages of starting from scratch are that you won't pay premium prices in the marketplace for going concerns, and you will be able to achieve maximum compatibility with your ongoing enterprises.

Score _____   **Running Score for Part IV** _____

                           Total Score for All Parts _____

━━━━━━━━━━━━━━━━━━━━━━━━━━━▶ **THE BOTTOM LINE**

A smooth interface between related operations may be worth more in the long run than money saved from eliminating start-up costs. General Motors is more likely to design and build its own plants than to try to convert a plant abandoned by Ford.

▶ ▶ ▶ ▶ ▶ ▶ ▶ ▶ ▶ ▶ ▶ ▶ ▶ So How Are You Doing?

The CEO has decided to send bottles of wine to his managers, based on how they did on Part IV.

If Your Score for Part IV Is	You Will Receive a Bottle of
▶ Over 65	A vintage Chateau Mouton–Rothschild
▶ Between 50 and 64	Taittinger Blanc de Blancs
▶ Between 30 and 49	An unpretentious imported burgundy
▶ Between 10 and 29	An unpretentious domestic burgundy
▶ Less than 10	Thunderbird

The Final Reckoning

In a rare display of uncommon good sense, the new administration has decided to award governmental managerial positions based not on your party loyalty and old-boy connections, but on how well you did with the problems in this book.

If Your Total Score Is	You Will Be Asked to Head
▶ Over 350	The Department of State
▶ Between 250 and 349	The Federal Reserve system
▶ Between 150 and 249	A Federal Reserve bank
▶ Between 50 and 149	The Bureau of Waste Reclamation
▶ Less than 50	The U.S. Post Office system

Index